HOW TO TURN YOUR DOG INTO A HORSE

The Option to Owning a Horse

VALERIE STANOL

 iUniverse

HOW TO TURN YOUR DOG INTO A HORSE
THE OPTION TO OWNING A HORSE

iUniverse books may be ordered through booksellers or by contacting:

iUniverse
1663 Liberty Drive
Bloomington, IN 47403
www.iuniverse.com
1-800-Authors (1-800-288-4677)

ISBN: 978-1-4917-3854-2 (sc)
ISBN: 978-1-4917-3855-9 (e)

Library of Congress Control Number: 2014910857

Printed in the United States of America.

iUniverse rev. date: 10/09/2014

Contents

Dedication

In loving memory of my first poodle, Bambi.

Acknowledgements

It is certain that the contents in this book would never have appeared were it not for the crazy series of events called my life. For this I must be thankful primarily for my parents. It was they who not only tolerated my incessant childhood rants and raves about horses, but encouraged my independent streak which allowed me to pursue my dreams. They encouraged me to experience the love of many different types of animals, which I now realize is the one undeniable and priceless gift to enable any child or adult to realize the capacity of their heart.

I must also thank my brother, Tony Stanol, for his constant patience as we grew up together. It was he who had to deal with the stinky small animal cages, he who was relegated to cleaning up Bambi's outdoor bathroom, and he who in our teenage years sacrificed himself to make the hundreds of trips to drive me to my horse's stable, even though he would have chosen to take his girlfriend out on a date in his new car. I know how sick it must have made him feel to cart me around until I got my driver's license, especially during all those return trips from the stable as I scuffed up his white carpeted car mats with my dirty boots, and infused his white vinyl seats with that special aroma of horses. Such is the dilemma of anyone carrying the horse-loving gene growing up amongst non-horse-loving people.

I'd also like to thank my sister-in-law, Karen Paul Stanol, who took the time out of her busy life schedule to provide me with her wonderful professional and personal editing. With her animal-loving background and her understanding of mine, she was able to provide some unique insight and creativity that I would have otherwise overlooked. I am very grateful for the constant and enthusiastic support she and my brother provided over the years in my pursuit of this book. Without them, I could never have completed this venture.

I must also thank all of my long-gone riding teachers throughout the years who supported me, yelled at me, but ultimately encouraged my passion and insisted that I get back on that horse, whether my dismount was intentional or not.

Lastly, for all of the hundreds of pets I've known, all of which I've loved, I must somehow show my thanks for enriching my life in the best possible way.

Introduction

Is there anyone out there who doesn't know of a horse-crazy person? That certain someone who has been obsessed with owning a horse but due to circumstances beyond their control was unable to have one? What is it about some people who yearn to experience that beautiful, powerful animal and connect with them? Volumes of books have been written about the love we have for horses. It's not the objective of this book to try to understand or explain that love. Instead I would like to offer a new approach for enhancing the bond between Animal and Human, another method to build a deep connection with your special friend.

What do many little girls answer when you ask them what they want for their birthday? "A pony." Imagine the look on a child's face when someone walks a pony up to them and says "Happy Birthday." It has been portrayed in books, movies, advertisements, etc. Everyone understands the ecstatic reaction of that child on seeing the biggest dream in their life come true. But that's only the tip of the iceberg. The child's horse passion seeps into their dreams at night with an ever-playing video of them riding their beautiful steed in wild abandon, freely in an open, grassy field with the sun shining. All is right with the world. It has got to be the number one wish of many youngsters. How often is that wish overlooked by frazzled parents? What are the ramifications of this? How often do we do anything and everything but get that child a horse? People grow up, have kids of their own, and often find that their very own children go through the same thing. They think, "Oh, sure. I went through that." It's all too common, and in some people that dream carries over into adulthood. Some parents are fortunate to understand what their children are truly experiencing, and have the finances to give them riding lessons or even their very own horse. Then they might live vicariously through their children or they might finally get to live their own long-lost dream themselves. However, as a riding instructor, I've found that starting to ride later on in life has its own set of challenges. Children tend to be more fearless starting out with some dangerous horse activities. I have found that adults seem to wear a veil of fear while working around and on a horse that doesn't exist in horse-loving children. That fear is easily sensed by horses, and this can work against the natural progression in learning. The best, safest option is to start horse-loving activities early using baby steps. Learning how to work with a horse in a safe, completely controlled environment sounds impossible, but it is definitely attainable. This book will give you a good start. Working with your dog will give you a great foundation in knowing what to expect and how to react, all of which is directly applicable to working with horses, but with none of the danger.

My family couldn't understand that horsey passion of mine. None of them had been known to have even the slightest inclination toward "that four-legged beast."[1] My roots sprang from the horseless city streets of Philadelphia where my parents were raised. They moved across the river to 1950s suburbia in New Jersey, into a tract home typical of Middle America. It wasn't zoned for horses, but to a young girl that didn't matter. My backyard looked huge to me, certainly big enough for a horse, or so I convinced myself with my dreams of jumping a steed over the birdbath, trotting him around the perimeter of the yard amongst the trees, and of course taking care not to trot on the hard concrete patio -- I already knew that would hurt his hooves! My father was a sheet metal worker, often fabricating heating and air conditioning ductwork at home. He also built a handy brick extension to our garage – in my eyes, the perfect structure for a horse stable! I tried to convince him that it was the appropriate size for a horse, but when that suggestion failed, I told him my second choice was our side patio which could easily fit a standing stall and grooming area. I promised to keep it clean and to tidy up after my horse every single day. Didn't I manage that with my gerbils, hamsters, canary, guinea pig, bunny, snake and hermit crab? Being repeatedly denied my biggest wish in the world, to have a horse, only made my fervor grow. Somehow it turned into my obsession.

I'm a little ashamed to admit (well . . . not really) that I was relentless in my efforts to convince my parents how serious I was about having a horse of my own. I just felt incomplete without a horse. In other words, I tried with all my heart and soul to make them feel miserable for not allowing me to have a horse. Imagine a child in the backseat of a car driving through the countryside whining "Horsey, horsey. Oh, I sure do LOOOOVE horses. Hey, dad . . ." or "DON'T change that channel. There's a horse on the screen!" I owned as many Jane and Johnny West characters and toy horses as money could buy. They were my favorites. Eventually I had accumulated a fine assortment of plastic horses, always the first things I sought in a toy store, and created my own stable in the backyard. Back then they didn't have the nice, big toy barns you can find these days, so I used my imagination and what I had on hand.[2] Nothing could stop me! I tied long grasses around tree twigs stuck in the ground to create standing stalls and box stalls, plus fencing around a big riding arena, big enough for toy horses, that is. I dug trails in the lawn around my stables, making a great English countryside hunt course. My imagination was rich, seeing myself as the owner of my own riding school one day, then managing my little orphanage stables the next -- whichever I dreamed about the previous night. My toy horses could jump over the rocks I placed on a jumping course. They could gallop along the hunt trails and soar high over water obstacles. They were glorious, strong horses and our backyard was the world where I could make them do any and everything!

I'm sure my parents prayed that their great investment in my toys would quell my ambition, but that was for naught. Their child still whined in the back seat, still pined at the dinner table, still insisted on watching every horse-related TV show, and generally drove them crazy. What was a parent to do?

And why is it that having a horse seems so impossible and unobtainable for so many? Too expensive? Too big? Too smelly? Too dangerous? Too time-consuming? Too remote? Too much responsibility? Nah! Personally, I don't think so. I'm certainly not rich, but I've been blessed to have experienced horses of all sizes, shapes, ages and talents throughout my lifetime, thanks to my never-ending motivation.[3]

That was the key! Inexplicable internal motivation. So here's my first bit of secret advice. To Kids: Never give up![4] Your parents may someday just cave in and buy you a horse, or at least agree to buy some riding lessons for you. And to Parents: There are hundreds of horsey toys out there which are bought for children in the hopes of placating children's wishes. I still have some from my childhood days. Buying all the toys in the world just isn't going to feed the child's need. The inevitable result is that the child's interest in such a gift is too short with the child reverting back to wanting a real, live animal. The dismal cycle of want, frustration, hope and appeasement inevitably repeats itself. Here's your chance to let the buck stop here: Focus on your own family dog.

I grew into adolescence without wavering from my goal. My parents realized that I was unlike a normal girl my age. Normally, little girls morph from being horse crazy into swapping horses for boys. Not me. I wouldn't back down from my dream. Begrudgingly, they granted me horseback riding lessons when I turned 10, the beginning of the Golden Years. I can still remember everything about my early days at the stable. The clippity-clop of hooves on the stable's cement floor, then that sound turning into muffled, regular clopping steps when walking the horses out of the barn. The snorting, the gentle, exhaling "pbshpbshpbsh" sound when horses cleared their noses. Sounds of tails swishing, hay munching, the deep breathing of relaxed horses. The different smells of timothy hay, alfalfa hay, straw, sweet feed. The wonderful, luscious smell of good leather in the tack room, of saddle soap and leather oils. And yes, even the sweet, earthy smell of manure. Only bonafide Horse People can appreciate that. They also remember their Golden

Years, when they started first working with horses, their first ride, their first jump.

My riding lessons continued for 5 years. Some of the other kids from my early classes dropped out, fewer still got their own horses, but nobody else kept just taking lessons for 5 years. Eventually I was given the more experienced horses, the larger horses or was the one asked to ride bareback when they ran out of saddles in larger classes. Yes, I feel I went as far as I could go at that stable, without owning my own horse.

But I continued to grasp at the straws of my ultimate dream, trying to immerse myself in horse ownership without actually having a horse. I already had the riding outfit. I had saved enough money to buy my first saddle. I kept hoping my parents would agree to let me have a horse to go under that saddle if I were serious enough to actually buy it. I found one in the Pennysaver, a Borelli English jumping saddle that cost $35; cheap, but basically intact and safe. Then my father softened just a little. He gave me his version of the horse he felt they could afford. It was a four-legged wooden and sheet metal horse he had made, without a head, sort of a half-barrel kind that I could set my saddle on. Fortunately, it was strong enough to handle my weight when I saddled it up and jumped on. I spent hours in that saddle, à la Elizabeth Taylor in "National Velvet," dreamy eyed and riding the imaginary horse. I'm sure that was the turning point for my parents, when they finally realized they had a crazy kid on their hands, and that it would be cheaper in the long run to buy her a horse rather than go the therapist route.

And so it happened. My dream came true when I was 15. I could share literally thousands of horse stories with my reader here relating to that and the rest of my life with horses. Suffice it to say that those brief 18 months with my penny-red chestnut Tennessee Walker gelding were among the most supremely happy times of my life. And that time was only the beginning of my lifelong passion for horses.[5]

So now you know where I began – I'm one of those with the Horse-Crazy Gene. It's ingrained in me for life. And if you also have that gene, you probably already know that horses are a large part of your identity. Seeing so many others with the Horse-Crazy Gene spurred me to write this book to help fulfill the needs of the horseless. And, more importantly, to offer an alternative.

Have you ever noticed a lonely little dog, sitting or sleeping, perhaps even forgotten, in someone's backyard? That little fellow needs exercise! It's commonly accepted knowledge that all living creatures need exercise. Without it, our muscles shrivel, fat accumulates and bones become brittle.

I personally cringe at the sight of a beautifully coiffed and otherwise handsome poodle waddling down the street, carrying far too much weight. If only that well-intentioned owner could trade in the bejeweled collar for regular exercise, not just a monthly walk, they would both benefit. Many bone, joint, heart problems, diabetes and cancer can be reduced or eliminated with exercise. The need is there, and it seems a dog's only goal in life is to spend time with people and simply do whatever their owners ask of them. Logically, dogs would be only too happy to exercise, if their owner took a little time to show them how.

With the new goal of training a dog to be a horse, a child with the Horse Crazy Gene will benefit immensely, as will their parents and siblings! Parents will notice their child opting for outdoor time rather than sedentary computer time. Dogs will relish the attention and love they start receiving from their trainers and will inevitably become more fit. Given time, a horseless person will gain the responsibility and fulfillment of training an animal. I've noticed that the more work you put into an animal, the more you naturally bond with it as it becomes a part of you, and you have yourself to thank for the progress. An unseen, long-term benefit will be the training knowledge horseless people will gain from learning many of the routines working with their dog-turned-horse. There are virtually no life-threatening dangers of working around dogs compared to horses. Ultimately, these techniques are also easily transferred to a horse, giving the reader a head start, when their dream of working with real, live horses comes true. In the meantime, and last but not least, it's cheaper to work with a dog than a horse.

At the very least, even if you don't actively follow this book as a guide, reading it will certainly let you appreciate your dog all the more, how it moves like a horse, jumps like a horse, but doesn't eat like a horse. It also doesn't smell like a horse, but don't try using that argument with bonafide horse people – they really want to live in a barn and prefer that equine aroma to perfume!

CHAPTER I

Do you know someone who is pining for a horse?

Think of Elizabeth Taylor in the movie, "National Velvet." It's a syndrome well known among young females, but is found universally in all ages and genders. Dealing with it can be frustrating for all involved. The horseless person is internally driven to be around horses, but those untouched by this syndrome find it hard to understand and might even fear being sucked into a hobby they just don't care for. Common in the horseless person is the innate love for all animals. But there is just something about the horse that's simply tantalizing more than any other animal. It's actually a very natural attraction and should not be discouraged. Teaching children how to properly handle domestic and/ or farm animals is invaluable in learning respect, sensitivity, responsibility and self-fulfillment. Teaching empathy to a young child is priceless as the child grows and develops socially. A sensitive heart is a rare jewel and if cultivated as a youngster, will carry over into the adult years. I personally feel an immediate kinship with anyone who shows they are truly an animal lover, that I can trust them as I know they have a sensitive heart.

And all this brings me to the point of this book. A dog is a fantastic substitute for the interaction Horse Crazy people are looking for! Before I finally (and I mean FINALLY!!) got my wonderful Tennessee Walker horse, Bambi came along. Yep. My world opened up the day my parents brought home Bambi, a 10-pound, black miniature poodle. Bambi was the "runt" of the miniature litter with a white spot on his chest. He wasn't the Best of the Best poodle in the world, but what he had was a good poodle build, intelligence, pluckiness and beautiful movement. In fact, his movement reminded me of a horse. His legs were long like a horse. And he could trot like a horse! I remember teaching him to jump over my leg. A light must have come on somewhere in my brain that he could actually jump *better* than a horse. His intelligent poodle mind was capable of learning a myriad of tricks. "Sit, Bambi. Lie down, Bambi. Give me your paw, Bambi. Good dog, now put it down. Now gimme the other paw. Now both paws. Good dog, Bambi!" It took me awhile, but I noticed when I'd take Bambi for walks on a leash, he'd follow alongside at my particular pace, just like a horse. This wasn't rocket science, but a starting point for my hypothesis: In my young mind, I figured out that dogs move like horses, dogs jump like horses, dogs are alive, horses are alive so dogs are just like horses. Logically, I proceeded to turn Bambi into the closest approximation of a horse that I could get. I was lucky that my parents had brought home a poodle: The breed happens to have an unusually high IQ along with other physical benefits. I believe this makes them the ultimate choice in dog breeds for simulating a horse.

Which brings me to my next point:

CHAPTER II

Is your dog suitable?

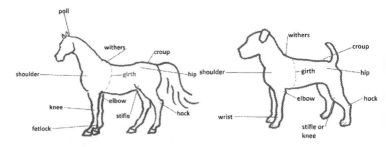

Let's take a look at how similar dogs and horses are physically. They both have hair, well most of them. (Have you ever seen a hairless Chinese Crested dog?) They both have a long-ish back. They both have a tail. They both walk on 4 legs. They both have similar gaits. (The walk, trot/pace and canter/lope are explained later.) They are both intelligent and beautiful breeds.

There are some dog breeds that resemble horses more than others with longer legs, and quicker responses and gaits; however just because a dog is very small or even has short legs does not mean it can't move like a horse. Its movements will be quicker, but just as pretty. Some breeds, in general, are really not as suitable for doing what is outlined in this book. The "lumbering" breeds, breeds that move slowly or very low to the ground (think Basset hound) will not be as successful in attaining a close similarity to a horse that we are aiming to achieve, but it certainly doesn't mean you can't try with them. The lumbering breeds might be better when trained to pull a tiny cart or take on a trail ride, but not in fast-paced activities. Poodles, however, are the perfect example (I am a bit biased having loved them my whole life) of a breed that will excel in "turning into a horse" in every way.

The breeds that most resemble a horse physically are the best to turn into a horse. The perfect breeds have longer legs and a leaner skeleton. For instance, imagine a greyhound and a horse running side by side. They are very similar, as opposed to a Daschund and a horse. However, with a stretch of the imagination, all dogs have the capacity to move in a manner similar to a horse. But what if your dog isn't the perfect breed for your horse-related intentions? What if he doesn't move like a horse? What if he's just too lazy? What if he's a bit too pudgy (at first)? Just keep trying! You are both bound to improve in health and vigor, as well as bonding in the process. But if in the end this book doesn't work for your dog, just try using the techniques on another one who's more suitable, like a poodle.

There are some obvious physical differences between horses and dogs that should be addressed as well. Unless you consider a very small breed of horse, like a Shetland pony, for instance, you can safely assume all dogs will be smaller than horses. The backs of horses aren't as flexible as dogs, but they are much more strong, which is why you can ride a horse but not a dog. Dogs' backs are not built to hold any weight, so never sit on a dog. Also horses have a very unique set of teeth with a natural opening, that is no teeth, between their front incisors and their molars. The bars of their gums are actually toothless for a couple of inches their on the sides of their upper and lower jaws. It's where the "bit" part of a bridle lies, in their mouth, over their tongue. Dogs do NOT have that opening between their teeth, so they are completely unable to close down on a bit in their mouth without the bit banging against and breaking their teeth, so never put anything like a bit into a dog's mouth. Dogs and horses have very different feet and, when it comes to speed, in general dogs aren't as fast as horses. I'll cover some specifics on this here:

Feet: Horses and dogs have completely different feet. Horses have hard, one-piece hooves, and dogs have flexible paws with digits and soft pads. Horses wear metal shoes to help keep their hooves from splitting apart so must be worked on soft footing such as softer dirt to allow their hoof to grab into it and assist in their movement. It's also helpful in protecting their joints as the soft ground provides cushioning. Horses do not do well on hard ground such as paved roads without wearing special rubber shoes fitted on their feet. They can also slide around on pavement if they wear metal shoes, and do not have the same reflexes as a dog to get back up should they fall. Dogs, on the other hand, can run on hard or soft ground without shoes or padding, although sometimes people put little booties on their feet if the pavement is hot or rocky. The flexible pads on the bottoms of their paws gives them better grip in making sharp turns.

The legs of horses and dogs may look similar in that there's one in each corner of their body, but they actually move differently. Because the horse has a hoof connected to a flexible ankle (fetlock joint), the horse will have a springier mechanism to its gait, even if his knee is locked. Dogs have wrists where a horse's fetlock would be, but the wrists lock up straight when they walk, giving them more stick-like movement, so the front of the body of a dog will feel more impact on hard surfaces. In the hindquarters, both dogs and horses have "hocks" which are similar to a human ankle joint. The angle in hocks allows a certain amount of spring, helps provide propulsion and assists in movements like jumping and stopping. If the natural conformation of either a horse's or a dog's front or hind legs points their legs out to the side, there is the concern that the joints could break down with a lot of movement, or hard, quick movements, so check with your vet as to its ability to sustain consistent exercise.

Backs: Obviously, since the horse is bigger, their back will be stronger. The dog's back is similarly shaped, but is not designed to carry weight so you should never, ever sit on a dog's back. And that means Never. Did I say never? Horses also have "withers," which is the hard, bony prominence between their back and their neck, the top of what we consider their shoulder area. That is where the height of both a horse and a dog is measured. The withers are much more prominent and pointed in horses because it is actually part of their backbone. In dogs, the withers are actually the tops of their shoulder blades. It's one reason why a saddle will naturally fit better on a horse; the withers prevent saddles from slipping forward, and help keep them in the middle or lowest part of the back. Since the shoulder area on a dog doesn't have this natural ridge, and because some dogs' backs are rounded upwards, only special saddles equipped with extra straps should be used for dogs.

Before you even begin to work with your dog as you would a horse, stand back and start to appreciate how he looks compared to a horse. What kind of horse breed could he be? Look at his coloring. A palomino (golden)? An Appaloosa (spotted)? A Paint (different patches of color)? Look at his general size. Could he be a draft horse, like the Budweiser draft horse? Or is he more like a tiny miniature size horse like a Shetland pony? Imagine him as a horse cavorting in a pasture, even if he is just running or walking around your living room. If he is lying down on his side, imagine how he would look as a horse lying down in a thick grassy pasture taking in the sun. Laugh when he jumps up on your couch because a horse would never do that!

Now onto Training!

It's important to note that everyone has a different relationship with their dog. Some see their pets as family, some only see them once a day to feed them. The happiest dog is one who has a working relationship with its owner. Dogs have been trained for centuries to work alongside people, and the more obedient types survived and thrived. They pleased people in the work they did, like sheepdogs, so people started selecting the ones they preferred. Dogs became man's best friend because of this, and branched off very specifically depending on what man required him to do. Therefore, all domestic dogs naturally want to work for us. Also, the more you work with your dog, the more you have yourself invested in him. You can't take credit for a ready-made dog if you didn't teach him anything. Your bond will inevitably grow stronger the more goals your dog reaches due to your training.

A good start is to teach your dog some tricks. This will build their confidence as the dog learns to take commands and it lays the foundation where they are to look to you for guidance. Most dogs want to please you if they can trust you to be the leader and teaching them tricks builds a small foundation to begin turning them into your horse.

I personally like to first teach my dogs to simply give me their paw. I start off bribing them with treats, but dogs can easily learn to take advantage of that and may only perform a trick for a treat. To get past that, start off with treats, but then slowly stop using them. Instead, praise your dog like he's the best dog in the world for performing for free! Other tricks can be learning to sit, lie down, stay, come, roll over and play dead (roll over halfway to their back). I hesitate to teach a dog to jump up for a treat or to learn how to bark. They often too easily perform these two tricks at the most inappropriate times, like when guests visit your home.

Try to remember that in training your dog to do anything, you must consistently use the same tone of voice, the exact same words, and the exact movement of your body. That is only if he responds to what you are trying to teach him. If he does not respond, do not to keep repeating the words over and over and over without any reaction from your dog. This could desensitize him to your words. Do remember to give him time to think, to sort things out. Don't expect an immediate response at first. It might just take him a few seconds to think about what you want. Be patient, but if he doesn't respond after you ask him the first time, you must up the game a little. Try using body language to convey your request. For instance, if he doesn't give you his paw when asking "Give me your paw," look down at his paw and ask again. If he still doesn't give you his paw, try picking up his paw and say "Give me your paw." (Yes, you might have to actually physically show him how.) Then reward him with a treat and praise him with happy, peppy words. I personally like the "helium voice," or talking to him in baby talk like people talk to little babies. (My poodles always respond to that!) Most dogs want to do what you ask as they want to be praised (or get a treat in the beginning), so they'll do their trick. Remember, if you act happy, your dog will think he's responsible for that and be happy, too. If you act disappointed, your dog will sense that and try harder because he now feels responsible for making you unhappy. (This is also why dogs usually resemble their owners – not just physically, but emotionally!) Be patient, though, and never, ever lose your temper with him. Remember, you are the one they are supposed to look up to. You are the Alpha (but not a mean Alpha). Keep in mind your body language as you train. Dogs in particular are sensitive to eye contact. Some more submissive dogs turn away from a constant stare. You will have to see how your dog responds to this, but remember if you are serious about something in particular, remember you can use your eyes and body language to convey and reinforce your commands.[6]

You will begin to develop your understanding of your dog's personality and learning capacity. Another way to get in touch with your dog is to learn to groom him like a horse is groomed. The main difference here is that dogs prefer to sit or lie down when at rest, unlike horses who stand up most of their day. When grooming a horse, he is standing up and is usually tied to a very secure object fixed in position that won't move if the horse pulls away for any reason. Horses are extremely strong and if a horse suddenly pulls back, a pole or fixed object can break away. The horse's natural instinct is to run away but they could drag the object along with them, frightening the horse even more, leading to a possible disaster. Dogs may have that same reaction, so it's also important to tie them to something that won't break away, even though they don't have quite the same strong instinct to pull away suddenly. Eventually, your dog should enjoy being groomed so much that he will stand in one place. Be patient until you get to this point where your dog stands still, not sitting down, not lying down. If he does sit or lie down, pick him up and say "Stand" firmly, but only say it once and look intensely at him to reinforce your command. Once he stays standing, say "Good dog" and continue grooming.

Your dog may or may not need the same kinds of grooming tools that a horse needs. Different breeds of dogs have different grooming needs, and require different brushes. Currying with a curry comb, a hard rubber brush with teeth, is generally the first step in grooming a horse. It really is not necessary to use on a dog unless he has rolled in the mud, which needs to be removed, or if it has been a very long time since he was last groomed, or his hair is shedding excessively. Currying is generally done in circular motions all over the animal's body, EXCEPT on the face and the legs since that could hurt if you accidentally ran the hard brush over a bony prominence. The next step is the dandy brush or stiff-bristled brush. Some dogs need a wire brush to get down to the skin, so don't skip this step. This type of brushing will remove the dirt and scurf out of the coat, bring the oils up from the skin through the hair to condition it and make it glisten, as well as massage your dog, which is the best part of grooming from your animal's point-of-view. Just use whatever brush your breed requires, such as a short-bristled brush for a Chihuahua or a slicker brush for a poodle.

With your dog standing, ready to be brushed, start at his head. Most dogs are fine with you beginning at their head. Some horses, on the other hand, are "head shy," meaning they pull away, throw their heads up, or are frightened to have their head touched or handled. This could be because they were mishandled when younger, or just never handled at all. Whether you have a relaxed or head-shy pet, the most important thing here is that you really need to gain their complete trust. The animal absolutely must know that you will not hurt it, will not scare it, and will not surprise it by touching it without warning. I like to sing to my dogs (and horses) to help them relax. They see I am relaxed and if they trust me, they will also relax. Singing actually also helps me to relax even more if I am apprehensive about doing something wrong.[7]

If your dog is sensitive about having any brush around his head, just desensitize that area with your hand. Let him see your hand coming, never surprise him by suddenly petting him on the top of his head (which is too aggressive for some dogs), but swing your hand slowly in front of his eyes and pet him slowly from front to back, over the top of his muzzle toward his neck. After a few times he'll get used to that and then you can brush him. Be extremely cautious when brushing near the animals' eyes and ears. It would be better to use a soft towel rather than a grooming tool as these areas are very sensitive, both in dogs and horses.

Keep in mind that horses and dogs also see much differently. Horses cannot see directly in front of them, or directly behind them. For instance, if you bring your hand up from below a horse's chin to his face, right in front of his face, to pat him on his forehead, you could easily frighten him because he will not be able to see your hand coming. (And by the way, please don't pat a horse on the nose. They just don't like it. Imagine someone coming up to you and patting you on your nose. Doesn't feel good, does it?) Keep the horse's eyesight in mind constantly, such as when you walk up to one. Never, ever approach a horse from behind as you could surprise it and the horse could kick you in a split second. You won't even see that hoof coming. Always start talking to a horse to let him know you are approaching, and keep more than an arm's length distance from its hind end, his kicking feet.

A dog's eyesight is somewhat different than a horse's. Most dogs have vision like ours. They can see in front of themselves and, to a limited extent, to the side, but they really have to turn their heads around to see behind them. Horses, on the other hand, only have to turn a little to the side to see behind him. Fortunately, dogs don't kick people like horses can, and even if dogs did, it wouldn't hurt. Both horses and dogs bite though, so be very careful to be nice to your dog so he doesn't resent the grooming. When approaching a dog's head, your approach will be more acceptable from the front as opposed from above. Patting the top of a dog's head is a sign of aggression. Whenever you meet a new dog for the first time, and you absolutely know the dog is not aggressive, you may "ask" him to be your friend as you extend your hand to him with your

Palm Up and scratch him under his chin or neck. Do not pat him on the head as no one, neither dog nor humans, really likes that. Horses also prefer that you scratch (not pat) their cheeks and, again, do not pat the nose. Their cheeks are just itchier. ALWAYS think of the Animal's point-of-view. [8]

While grooming your dog, brush down the neck, in the direction of hair growth, with the hair tips pointing towards the tail. Then continue to brush over their backs, again without pushing down too hard as parts of their backs are very sensitive. Use this grooming time as an opportunity to examine and evaluate where he likes to be groomed, and if he is actually painful. You'll be doing the same with a horse some day, and if you find an area that is suddenly sore, you must look into the possibility that he could be sick or lame. Remember to keep talking to your dog to reassure him throughout the process. But also remember not to keep repeating commands, like stay, or relax. If you repeat commands too much, it desensitizes the animal and they tune you out so that those words mean nothing. When you do give a command, however, do it with sufficient authority and confidence so your dog feels it. And make sure you get the response you want. Don't let your animal ignore you.

The next step with a horse is combing or brushing the mane or tail, but unless you have a Chinese Crested breed, you can skip this step in a dog. Personally, I don't like to comb out a horse's mane and tail too often as this can pull out hairs (which take a long time to grow back) and make them look ragged. If a horse's mane and tail are long you should use a detangler first to minimize hair damage. If you have a long-coated dog and the fur is too thick or matted, a good grooming in the hands of a professional will get you off to a good start, but it's your responsibility to keep your dog looking good, so regular grooming maintenance is necessary. If you stay on top of regular brushing, your dog's coat will be guaranteed to look its best, and more importantly, your dog will be feeling his best as you can reach a lot of his itchy spots. It's good practice to groom thoroughly before any workout for this reason – it puts your dog in a positive frame of mind. You will also need to decide if the coat of your dog is suitable for lots of exercise. It should not be too long if exercising outside in the summertime. (See Chapter III for specific directions on how to monitor your dog during exercise.)

Lastly, check your dog's feet. Horses' hooves are picked out. This means that dirt can get trapped on the underside of a hoof, and a hook-like hoof pick is used to pick out the dirt with one hand while the hoof is being held with the other. You can pretend to pick out your dog's feet, but do not use a pick as the skin between their pads is soft and very sensitive. Do, however, remove pieces of debris, burs or stickers that might make walking painful for them.

CHAPTER III

Starting out

First of all, your dog must be leash trained. In horses, this is called "working in-hand." The goal of proper leash training is a completely obedient dog who will stay by your side at whatever speed you are going, who will not pull away, not try to play or grab the leash, not try to run in front of you and will not lag behind you.

To start leash training you must first practice how to properly hold a long lunging rope. This is a soft nylon rope, $\frac{1}{2}$ inch in diameter with a snap on the end, at least 20 feet long. You should start with the end opposite the clip. It's helpful to

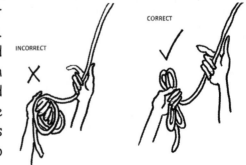

INCORRECT

CORRECT

tie a knot in the opposite end you will be holding so it will not slip completely out of your hands. Hold that end with your left hand and pull the rope through your right hand about 2-3 feet and make a big loop by putting the end of the rope in your left hand. Keep repeating this, making more loops until you have only a few feet between your left hand and the clip to snap onto dog's harness. This last straight length of the rope should be enough to keep the rope slack between you and the dog most of the time, but short enough that you are able to make a connection to the harness very quickly, about 2 feet. You should end up holding several large loops in your left hand while walking your dog. Try to keep these loops very organized and of the same size in your left hand so you do not let them drop to the ground. If they fell to the ground, you could easily trip and fall over the rope or you could jerk on your dog's line, hurting him. It's easier than you think for those loops to tangle. If they do, or if you happen to drop a loop or two, stop your dog as soon as you can, make him stand still so you can fix those loops. A top priority should be keeping that rope organized into even loops. You will be very thankful you learned to do this from the beginning especially when it comes time to train an animal many times your weight.

At this point, we can actually begin to work with your dog, but something must be repeated. **One of the most important things to remember about training an animal is to Never continuously repeat a command over and over if they don't seem to understand. If after a couple of times your dog doesn't get it, use another strategy to help him learn. You may not be making yourself clear or may be doing something wrong so that he just doesn't understand. Repeating the voice commands will desensitize your dog to that command, and above all, they will lose their trust in you, breaking down your connection with them. If they don't understand when you ask them once, try once more, but never more than that. Instead either go back and perform something they do remember to fortify their trust and confidence, or try another way to show them exactly what you want. You have options, and as the trainer, it's up to you to learn them. You will get to know what works with your dog the more you work with him; you could possibly raise the pitch of your voice or use some other bodily command. Good training does not happen overnight, so please be patient, don't allow him or yourself to become frustrated. Just take a deep breath, and never hesitate to ask for help from someone else. The process of learning should be happening both for you and your dog.

Leash training can take place indoors or out. To get started, you'll need to assess your living environment and what you have on hand. Outside, of course, you have more area to work in. A yard or level ground with short grass is ideal. It provides excellent traction and cushion for dogs. A dirt yard will do, but it is dusty and can scratch a dog's tender, fleshy paws. Concrete is not the best as again, it's abrasive and very hard on an animal's joints. One alternative you do have with your dog that you don't have with a horse is bringing your dog indoors - great for bad weather when it's too hot, cold or wet outside. You'll need a room big enough for your dog to circle within, depending on the size of the dog. This could range from a cleared area 8 x 8 feet around for dogs less than 20 pounds, to 12 x 12 feet around for a larger dog. Carpeting is better than vinyl, wood, or other slippery surface. Obviously, any furniture that could be in the way should be temporarily moved to make that area completely clear. I used to walk my dog all over my house, pretending I was riding on a horse trail in a forest pretending the furniture was trees and boulders. (I would lead my dog to the stream of water in the sink, but he wouldn't always drink.)

In your chosen area of exercise, put the harness on your dog and prepare the rope as described above. You will be leading your dog on his left (or near side). When you lead a dog, your right arm needs to be closest to his left shoulder, just like when leading a horse.[9]

You'll need to position your dog with his body pointing forward, standing still. You can reinforce that position with the command "Stay." You also need to keep your body pointing forward, not facing your dog, in order to start out walking in the correct direction. As you are both facing forward at the standstill, you must first say "Walk" and then walk forward, hoping your dog will follow you. You must verbally give the command first before taking a step so that he learns to really listen to what you say before doing something. This actually reinforces his trust in you. He might just stand there, or worse, sit down. If he does sit, gently pick him back up again and say "Stand." Go back to your original position and ask him to walk, then take your first few steps forward holding the rope firmly so that your dog gets the physical invitation to walk forward with you. If he does start walking, praise him a lot, but keep walking. The rope must be held so that you actually have a light contact with the dog through the rope. That is, the rope should not be very slack so that it hangs down between you and the dog, nor should you be constantly pulling on the dog so that he moves toward you.

Keep walking in a straight line for a minute or two. Before you intend to stop, say "Ho" and only then you may stop. This warns your dog before you actually stop that you intend to stop. The goal is to get him to stop straight forward in his tracks. Again, if he is listening to you, he should hear your command and also read your body language and should stop as well. At first, he may just keep walking forward, but if you are holding onto the rope, he'll end up pulling himself to a stop. You should Never, Ever pull back or jerk on that rope. You will lose his trust.

Handling the rope lightly will teach him to respond gently. In case he didn't stop when you did, his body might have turned around, facing you, or the rope may have tied around your ankles, so take care to reposition yourself, the rope and your dog to start this process once again. Remember, never lose your temper and always stay calm. Your dog notices your emotions and reactions and will feed off of them. In fact, he'll get anxious if you get anxious, and will feel happy when you let him know he has done a good job. It could take you five minutes, or a day, or a week, depending on the dog, the environment, and how much patience you have to completely master this first step of leash training. The more time you spend getting it absolutely perfect, the better the communication will become between you and your dog, and the better off your dog will be in the next step.

Depending on the size of dog you have, you may or may not be able to keep up with how fast your dog trots which is the next gait faster than the walk. Assuming you can, try running alongside him (or walk as he trots if he's a tiny dog) when he trots on the leash. Again, starting from a standstill with both of you facing forward, give the command "Walk" and then after walking straight forward for a while, give the command "Trot," spoken in an energetic way ("Teee-ROT!"). Then begin walking or running faster so that your dog must break into a trot. A trot is not a canter, a lope or a run, but is a two-beat gait where his front legs move in the opposite direction as his back legs. Try keeping a very light contact with the dog's harness as he trots. You should feel a quick give-and-take in the rope as the dog bounces a little bit at the trot, up and down, up and down. Once again, give the command to "Ho" and then slow down and come to a stop slowly. Do not slam on your breaks without giving the dog a chance to hear what you are planning on doing or else you'll break down his trust. He may take a few steps in the walk before stopping.

To change it up a little bit, do the same on the other, far side of your dog.[10] Position yourself on your dog's right side with his body facing forward, and use your left hand closer to him with your right hand taking up the loops of the rest of the rope. Try not to let him sit down. If he does sit, say "Stand." If you need to, point him in the correct direction by physically turning his body with your hands. Don't use the leash to pull him around. Your goal is to keep him at your left side and staying at whatever pace and direction you move. He should also keep his distance a foot or two away from your body. He should respect your place, just as a horse should respect your personal space. If a horse decides to step into that space, it is a sign of disrespect and you could be knocked over and hurt. A dog should learn to stay out of your space unless you invite him into it. If he chooses on his own to step into your space, or worse to jump up on you, this is rude behavior. He's trying to be the boss and you should remind him that you are the boss. To remind him of that, say the command, "Back" only once and step forward towards him into his space (without stepping on his toes). You should do this whenever he steps into your space. You, the Alpha, must remain in charge of your dog. Stay calm and don't get upset with him. If you ever do, he'll realize that he has some control over you. Remain consistent and patient. This will be even more important when you have a horse in the future. Remember, you are the Alpha, but to stay the Alpha, you must set a good, respectable example, one your dog can look up to and trust. Everything is based on that.

Before you start to walk forward, say "walk." In the beginning, you must give him a little notice (1-2 seconds) before you expect to see him walking. Later, he should walk immediately upon your command. If he ignores your command, make a kissing sound or click with your mouth to him like you would with a horse to get his attention. Dogs naturally want to do what you ask. You are the one in charge, but you should Never harshly tug at the lunge line. You may pull slowly and gently until there is a little contact with him through the lunging line, but you must also immediately release that pressure when your dog does begin to walk. That is his positive reward for doing what you want. Keep in mind that your goal is to only say your command once. Do not keep saying the word or your dog will ignore you. You must have his undivided attention. Be patient. It takes time for a good trainer to get immediate results with their commands, but the experience is extremely fulfilling. The goal is for your dog to walk whenever you ask him.

Your dog must wait for your command for anything. Do not allow him to walk when you simply walk forward without a verbal command. You must first indicate that you want something, first with your voice, and also with body language, so those two tools must be saying the same thing.[11]

Before you actually stop walking, you must again give your dog some notice. Say "Ho" with authority in your voice. Say it only once and then stop. If your dog keeps walking forward, simply let his own motion forward stop him. Do not pull back on the leash. Just hold your hand still and let him put the pressure on the halter by himself. Just remain motionless until he comes to a complete halt. Remember to release that contact once he stops. He should still be facing in the same direction as you. If he is not, bend down and fix his body to point forward in a standing position. Do not ask him to sit as sometimes dog trainers do. Horses don't sit when you lunge them, and neither should your dog during this exercise.

One of the techniques people use to exercise horses is called lunging. It is pronounced "lunj-ing", not with a hard "G" as in lungs, and definitely not "lounging."

It is an exercise you may have seen horses do (as in a circus) when the horse moves in circles in a round pen as the trainer stands in the middle of the circle. Please do not follow the specific lunging instructions of horse trainers when you are working with dogs, even though lunging helps both species. Horses are taught to lunge in a very different way with many trainers known as "horse whisperers." Those trainers use the specific instincts of a horse in ways that definitely do not apply to the dog. It looks like chasing a horse around the inside of a pen. In truth, it isn't really chasing but something that uses the horse's natural instincts to communicate in the horse's language. The dog's brain is not wired like this, so you will not be doing the same steps as the Horse Whisperer, but you will be using the dog's natural talents. Your dog should be very responsive with leash training and fully understand the commands to walk, trot, and stop (ho) before you actually continue onto lunging.

Lunging is a very useful exercise, but isn't only used to make a horse move or burn off steam. With lunging you can actually study and analyze your animal's movement while they exercise. Standing in the middle of a circle gives you a consistent, unchanging viewpoint as opposed to watching an animal run towards or away from you. This way you can observe how the animal is improving, if the animal is tired and if the animal is lame, etc. You also have more control while keeping your animal in constant, small turns than you would should he ever choose to bolt forward in a straight line. This way, you can closely watch how his body movement changes, speeds, up, slows down, turns in/out, etc., and how quickly he responds to your commands.[12] The movement of lunging requires more effort on their part because their two legs closest to you (the inside legs) don't move as far as the outside circle while turning, but their back should conform to the actual arc of the circle. This takes more concentration, balance and coordination, which is more difficult than just moving in a straight line.

You will need "tack" for lunging. Tack is the term used to describe a bridle and saddle or harness that you put on a horse. Dogs have collars, back harnesses, leashes, etc., but we're going to refer to it here as tack as that's the equine term. What you'll need for lunging purposes is a 20-foot-long, lightweight rope made of nylon or cotton, not more than 1/2 inch in diameter in larger dogs, and not more than $\frac{1}{4}$ inch in very small breeds. It needs to be lightweight so it doesn't get tangled and so it doesn't interfere with your dog's movement. A dog collar should never be used for lunging as a dog's throat is extremely tender and you can permanently damage their windpipe (trachea) and voice box so be sure to get a nice body halter which wraps around your dog's chest, similar to a bridle or halter that would be used on a horse's head. Some of these halters can be confusing to put on and adjust, but basically they are strips of material, nylon, leather or even cloth that wrap around and between the two front legs, up over the back and under the front of the chest. The attachment for the rope (leash attachment) should be a metal ring at the top over their backs. You may use more tack later on as your dog progresses in his stamina, but I will discuss that later in this book.

The harness needs to be attached around the chest so that the legs can move freely, that is not get caught inside the harness straps, and so that your dog can breathe deeply. It should only be tight enough so he cannot wiggle out of it. If you can easily insert two fingers between the harness and against his body at any point, this should allow enough for movement and breathing. Also make sure that if he is able to get his lower jaw under a strap and chew on the harness, especially the straps that are on the front of the chest, this could be dangerous. He might get his jaw stuck within the harness, so those straps might need to be more snug. It would be better also if you could allow your dog to get used to first wearing the harness without attaching the lunging rope. This could take a few hours but do not leave your dog unattended when you first put on the harness. Once your dog doesn't seem to notice wearing the harness, he will be comfortable enough to start lunging.

Lunging requires a safe area large enough for your dog to trot around in, and this, of course, depends on the size of your dog. Shorten the rope into loops in your right hand, and put your left hand about two feet away from your dog. You will be facing your dog and you will be walking sideways, to the left (counter-clockwise movement). Walk your dog in a big circle with him on the outside of that circle and you on the inside. Then increase the distance between you and your dog gradually, so that he stays on the outside of the circle. If he tries to come closer to you, you'll need to say "over" while pointing with your left hand to the outside of the circle and also his shoulder, and lead him back to the outside of the circle. Make your circle as close to a perfect circle as you can, not a square, not an oval, not an egg shape. Keep increasing the distance between you and your dog while increasing the length of rope until you find yourself in the middle of the circle with your dog walking around you. If he stops, tell him to "walk."

You are now applying your "aids," the things you use to control his movement, like your own voice or your body movement. Animals are more aware of your body movement or your "body language" than you think. Animals don't use their voices in the way we do. If you watch the eyes and even the ears of an animal, you can actually "read" what they are thinking. For instance, if an animal holds its head up very high, arching its back in the shape of a U, chances are that the animal is tense. The muscles in his back are working overtime, which isn't necessary in lunging. They could hurt themselves and you might have a more difficult time controlling your animal. So if you see your dog with his head up watching you with his back arched, you will need to be much more patient until he calms down and pays more attention to you. As soon as your animal relaxes, his back should swing, that is not be rigid, and his hind legs should be more effective in stepping up closer to his front legs, which would turn his back more into an umbrella shape. They call this "round" with horses. A rigid back is actually more easily visualized in horses; the top line of their back looks more like a U shape, and it looks like their neck is tense with their head held more high than low. You know what your dog looks like when he relaxes, so the ultimate goal here is that he moves forward easily and comfortably.

Your goal is that the animal gives you 100% of his attention. If he is distracted by a noise, sound, or another animal outside of your immediate area, you have lost your connection with him. Younger animals are more prone to distraction so they may need more time to learn how to consistently keep their attention on you, and you need to attempt to get their attention gradually, so just be aware of their body language. If they look to the outside of your area away from what they are doing, you can either call their name or whistle, so that they bring their attention back to where it should be, that is on you.

When you feel your dog is becoming more and more attentive, you'll need to teach him to stop on command at the end of your rope while lunging. When you say "Ho," step sideways in the same direction his head is pointing. That means if he is circling to the left of you, say ho and step to your left as if you are attempting to step into his path, even though you are far away from him. In body language, you are reinforcing your verbal command with your physical command. If he does not stop, very gently tug on the rope, but do not ever suddenly pull or jerk on the rope without warning him first to stop. Remember, this will decrease his trust in you and he won't behave. He always wants to please you, but not if you resort to tricking or hurting him.

When he finally does stop, loosen up the rope a little and praise your dog. If you want him to change directions, slightly put the rope in your other hand, say "come," indicating you want him to turn towards you, and point that hand in the opposite direction he was just moving and say "walk." He should then turn his body towards you, turn around and start walking the other way. You should also change the amount of times he walks around. At first, try walking nonstop for 3 circles, then halt, then 2 circles and stop. Also try stopping at different places so he doesn't anticipate stopping. Another word of caution: Always try to change up your training just a little every day. Dogs, just like humans and even horses, can get bored. You may be thrilled with your ability to get your dog to successfully learn these techniques, but if you repeat them too much, your dog will become bored. They could turn sour on the whole subject of what you're trying to do with him. Do try to show him how pleased you are with his progress, but don't repeat something too much once he finally does it successfully. Horses are more creatures of habit, but can also easily become bored.[13] Then if your dog performs a movement without your actually asking for it, it is actually a form of disobedience. Horses sometimes anticipate a movement that people always do with them at a certain time or a certain place. The consequences of this are obvious, especially if someone else is riding that horse. Dogs and horses must wait for your signal.

Once you have mastered the walk, ask for the trot and work within that gait, but again no more than a few minutes at first for a few days as it takes a lot of fitness to sustain movement in a circle. Asking for the canter could take a lot more on your part to get your dog cantering and keep him cantering. Just remember to activate your voice more, making it sound more energetic, like "CAN-terrrrrr!" If he breaks his gait down into the next slower one, reinforce your voice command. To use body language to reinforce his gait you will need to step energetically towards him to gain his attention, but try to aim your body toward the tail end of your dog, as that is his engine.

Take your time working in each of the three gaits. Remember, your dog is working a lot harder than you are when you lunge him, so don't over-work your dog. Sometimes all it takes is 5 minutes walking around in a circle to make your dog tired if he isn't in good shape. It does take lots of time to condition your dog, which means increase his stamina and fitness. Try to perfect all of these steps before moving on as your dog will be that much better when you do progress. No matter what, though, you will definitely see progress in both him and yourself. Share your enthusiasm with your dog. He needs to regularly and appropriately see how he is pleasing you.

It's a good idea to monitor the fitness of your dog. To do this, you'll need to record the vital signs ("TPR"=temperature, pulse or heart rate, and breathing or respiratory rate) of your dog before attempting any exercise, and then about once a week. Normal vital signs for a dog depend on the age and size of your dog. Check their heart rate while they are resting and before exercise. Do not check the heart rate at their neck as this could be dangerous, and that goes for people and horses, too. Pressing on a neck artery (the carotid sinus) signals the heart to slow down, decreasing the amount of blood to the brain. You'll need to place your hand against their chest just behind their left elbow to feel their heart beating. In a horse, you could sometimes see the pulse in a horse's neck without feeling for it. A horse's pulse can also easily be taken on the lower leg around their fetlock. Make sure that your dog stays still as any movement (in them or in you) might feel like a heartbeat. In thinner dogs, the heartbeat will feel like two tiny beats (lub-dub) with a pause, then two tiny beats and a pause, and so on. Those two little beats are actually counted as one beat or one cycle of a heartbeat. In average-weight dogs, you may only feel one heartbeat on the chest. Make note of his resting heart rate as you will compare this number to his heart rate after exercise.

Normal resting heart rate:

Large-breed dogs over 50 pounds:	70-120 beats per minute.
Medium-sized dogs 25 to 50 pounds:	80-120 beats per minute.
Small dogs from 10 and 25 pounds:	90-140 beats per minute.
Very tiny dogs less than 10 pounds:	100-160 beats per minute.

Keeping your hand on his chest, you can also check his breathing rate or respirations. At rest, he should take 15-30 breaths per minute. Respirations do two things in a dog. Not only do they bring in oxygen, but breathing also cools off a dog as they don't sweat during exercise like humans. Do not check your dog's respirations when he is panting, as he is most likely cooling off his body instead of replenishing oxygen needed after exercise. Initially checking their respirations will show you if your dog is having trouble breathing from the beginning. If it sounds like they are snorting or wheezing while at rest, have them checked out at the vet just to make sure that they don't have a medical condition that might prevent them from exercising or need to be treated first.

Also check your dog's temperature. Your dog's normal resting temperature can range normally from 100.5 to 102, higher than ours. It will temporarily increase after they exercise, so, like heart rate and respiration, only take the temperature when your dog is at rest. The most accurate way to take a dog's temperature is through the dog's rectum by someone who knows how to use a thermometer. If the temperature is higher than 102.5, the dog might have some disorder going on in their bodies, and again need to be seen by a vet for possible treatment.

Eventually, you will notice your dog becoming more fit. You will also notice a difference in the vital signs, the heart rate and respirations, of your dog. His resting heart rate may decrease at rest. That's normal. He may not work so hard at breathing once he becomes more fit. You will notice that he can exercise for longer periods without tiring, but remember, all this training should be done gradually.

Each dog will progress at its own rate of learning, as well as according to how patient and disciplined you are. A major consideration in this progress, however, is how physically fit your dog is. Remember to take it slowly at first, even if your dog is young, has a clean bill of health and has no bone or joint problems. If your dog is overweight, has not exercised much, or has a medical problem, especially relating to the heart, your veterinarian should approve your dog for exercise first. In the early stages you should limit a healthy dog's exercise to 15 minutes at a time. As an example, you might want to start with 15 minutes daily for one week, then increase to 20 minutes the next week, and then add 5 minutes each week after that. Exercising will help both you and your pet sleep much better at night, so don't forget to allow adequate time to rest!

CHAPTER IV

Disciplines

a. English

    1. Flatwork

    2. Dressage

    3. Jumping

b. Western

    1. Barrel racing

    2. Reining

    3. Trail obstacles

c. Driving

By now, your canine equine should be very familiar with moving to your command. If you feel he's ready to progress, you can start to learn a few of the many equine disciplines available to try with him. The four basic categories covered in this chapter will be English style (which is mistakenly called Eastern), Western style, Trail Riding and Driving, or pulling a cart. The dynamics of each style will help your dog flourish in different ways.

I would definitely suggest trying the disciplines in the order presented in this book -- English, Western, Trail Riding and then Driving. The English section contains the most information and forms the best foundation from which to go into the other two disciplines. Once you've accomplished the English discipline, then Western barrel racing could be a nice change, but it should not be tried unless you have complete control over your dog since they could hurt themselves or you. After that comes trail riding which is fun in that it's very relaxing and allows your dog to let his hair down and chill out from all the stuff you've been teaching him. Trail riding can be done both in English and Western styles. You never want to burn them out with too much information, so trail riding is often a nice change from a daily routine of close training, either with your dog or a horse. I saved Driving for last, as that one can be catastrophic if you can't thoroughly predict what your dog is capable of doing. The same relates to horses. If a horse isn't perfectly relaxed and able to focus and follow your commands completely, he could run away with you as he pulls the cart you are riding in. Learning English, Western and then Trail Riding will help you see what your dog reacts to and then allows him to incorporate his new knowledge into the dynamics of pulling an object. Please do not just hitch your dog up to something without training him thoroughly beforehand as you can cause irreparable damage.

Each breed of dog has a different way of moving, none better or worse, just different. Some dogs might have natural movement that exemplifies a dressage horse -- fluid, elastic and precise -- whereas other dogs may have a natural talent in jumping or being springy, athletic and agile. Still other dogs are naturally very mellow, preferring the couch to a jump. Each of these "types" can be matched to a particular discipline: A mellow dog would be best suited on the trail while a springy dog would best enjoy cross country jumping. The same goes for horses. Generally, skittish horses are not well suited to a leisurely stroll out on the trail, but better for barrel racing or English jumping. Try out each discipline with your dog and see which one he seems to enjoy the most. This will also help you develop your eye for watching horses at work. You'll eventually be able to learn to identify what a horse's natural physical and mental talents are when it comes time to buy your own. You'll also be able to more quickly notice the differences in conformation, movement and attitude that some horses have that make them better at one discipline than another. For instance, a horse with long legs can be naturally good at jumping, and a horse with shorter legs and a very strong hindquarter (engine) would be great at barrel racing. The same follows with your dog. Ultimately, their conformation matters because their skills can be a result of their build. There are exceptions to this concept in that some animals just love to participate in a certain discipline, even though they aren't built for it.

I once bought a beautiful chestnut Thoroughbred gelding that I had big plans for. He was going to be my first real dressage horse because I just loved the discipline, its beauty, grace and class. Dressage horses perform mostly in the ring, although they like to relax on the trail. However, there are ideal physical and mental traits that dressage horses should have, none of which my Thoroughbred had. I didn't realize that when I bought him. He loathed riding in the arena, which I love to do. He found it boring. He wasn't very mellow either, which is actually typical of most Thoroughbreds, and I preferred to go on long slow trail rides in the afternoon. You need a mellow horse for that. He did, though, have a big "engine" behind, in his hindquarters, which you'd think would be great for barrel racing. However, that's a Western discipline and I rode English. What was I going to do with this horse? Well, he absolutely loved, loved, loved to jump, but I didn't, didn't, didn't. He had so much energy and always "cleared" jumps, which means he jumped way over the jump, never hitting it or knocking it down. His form was beautiful and he had plenty of strength for it.

Unfortunately, I am scared to jump a horse. I'm an adult, and never like to take big risks. Jumping to me is a risky sport, and very difficult for adults to begin learning later in life. Despite my hunter/jumper background learned as a child while taking my first lessons, I never really felt comfortable jumping. In fact, my body is built more like a dressage rider's, tall, lean and with long legs. No wonder I love dressage. I'm built for it. Anyway, it finally occurred to me that my little Thoroughbred and I were just not meant for each other. Sadly, I eventually sold him and bought my first dressage horse, a Swedish warmblood, which was one of my all-time favorite horses in my life. Sure enough, her body was built for dressage with her long and balanced topline, long neck and long legs. She was also so smart, enjoying the mental challenges required for arena riding, and she was pretty good on the trail, too, as warmbloods are known to be more calm than thoroughbreds in general. If I had known then what I know now and the information contained in this book -- that is, how to develop your eye for conformation, movement and personality in both dogs and horses -- I could have saved my Thoroughbred and myself some heartache.

One basic question is: *What is the difference between English (below, left) and Western style (below, right)?*

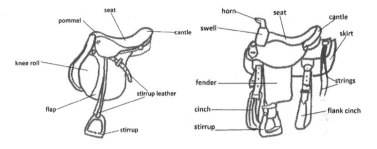

First of all, an English saddle is much smaller than a Western saddle, and the way one sits in each saddle is a bit different. English saddles do not have a "horn," which looks like a rounded knob or handle that sticks up from the front of the seat of a Western saddle. Instead English saddles have a rounded pommel in front. They sit more forward on the horse's back. Acquaint yourself with the different styles on the Internet or in your neighborhood if you're lucky to live near a stable just to see for yourself. I used to collect free horse tack catalogs just to look at the types of tack that horses need. I studied them over and over to see what options were available for different types of horses, different styles of riding, and just to acquaint myself with the terminology. There are many types of saddles to choose from, as well as other horse equipment. Each piece has a different function, and it's fun to learn about them all.

The ways people sit in each saddle are much different. There are types of English riding where the stirrup leathers (the long piece that attaches the stirrup to the seat of the saddle) are shorter, such as in racing and jumping. In dressage saddles, the stirrup leathers are the longest to enable the rider's legs to straighten out more to come down and around the ribs of the horse to increase the contact and feeling with the horse's body. In jumping saddles, the rider's stirrup leathers are much shorter which bends the rider's legs at the knee much more, enabling the rider to stand up clear of the saddle when going over jumps so the weight of the rider does not bump into the horse's body as they go over a jump, making it easier for the horse to move more freely. In Western saddles, the stirrups are attached to fenders, and the length is lower as it is more comfortable for the rider to keep a more straight leg, as in trail riding.

You were actually training your dog to "ride on the flat" (not jump, which is covered later) while you were lunging him. He learned how to walk, trot, canter and stop (halt) which is similar to the early work of a young horse. The next step in training is called tacking up, which means fitting your pet with a bridle and saddle. You have a few options for your dog. Available online are saddles made for dolls or toy horses that you could put on the back of your dog.[14] I would suggest measuring your dog first before you buy a saddle. From his withers (see Chapter II), measure half the distance to his tail. For dogs that are extra long in the back (the Dachschund, for example), measure one third of the distance. This is about how long the top of the saddle should be (from pommel to cantle). A saddle should be flexible, made out of rubber, neoprene, soft leather, or, best of all, fabric (I made my own as a child), so that it won't hurt your dog. The saddle will fit onto the front of his back, more towards the withers, not the middle of his back. You may also want to consider using some fleece, felt or other material that would cushion his back and keep the saddle from hitting his spine. Some dogs have more prominent spines (compared to horses) than others.

You will have to figure out the best way to keep the saddle on his back. Since you are probably still using a harness to connect your rope, you can just attach the saddle to the harness, although the saddle may bounce around when your dog trots and canters. To keep this from happening you could use elastic ribbon under his chest (a girth or cinch) to secure the saddle, and also a piece that goes on the front of your dog's chest, sitting just below the bottom of his neck in front, so that it does not slip backwards. (That chest piece is called a breast collar or martingale on horses.)

It might take your dog awhile to get used to having something attached to his back. Remember, the saddle should never be too heavy, and certainly not floppy as it could hit him in the head if it became loose.

Assuming you have him adequately tacked up, you are ready to ride, that is "ride your dog safely." **Remember, you should never ride your dog by sitting on him**. I know this whole book was written for you to learn how to turn your dog into a horse, but he just is <u>not</u> a horse, and <u>cannot</u> handle your weight. If you must ride, get on a horse, not a dog.

That being said, you could actually do the next best thing to riding your dog. To replace that rider, you will be using a rod or pole made out of very lightweight material, such as bamboo, a light, narrow wood pole like pine wood, or preferably a fiberglass pole like a fishing rod, with some soft, lightweight material like fleece wrapped around the end of it. As a child, I used a small, hollow, plastic toy broom. The bristles of the broom were soft enough to put on his back. By lightly placing the wrapped fabric, or the soft bristles onto the saddle, you are virtually riding your dog. You will now safely be able to feel through your hands and see from the side what it is like from a rider's point-of-view when your dog walks, trots and canters. At first, you will feel awkward trying to keep that pole from bouncing around (and hurting your dog if it bounces too hard), but when you learn how to ride a horse, you'll also have to learn how to work through that bouncing part, too. Resist the urge to actually attach any long pole to your dog's back. You can't use a seatbelt when you ride a horse, so don't cheat through this step with your dog. You do need to learn how to respond if the pole becomes unbalanced, just like you would if you were riding a horse.

When you first use the pole, your dog's natural instinct may be to pull away. If you don't know your dog's total history, he might be afraid of that pole if someone ever tried to hit him. A natural instinct in the horse is ingrained in their genes and goes back millions of years to when a horse learned to run away if something, like a wild mountain lion, were to jump on its back. Horses are flight (not fight) animals, and dogs have some of that instinct as well. You must teach your dog that you will not hurt him with the pole. Remember to never use that pole to discipline your dog. Never, ever hit him with it. If he gets hurt, you have yourself to blame, and you have ruined his trust. If he is afraid of it at first, let him examine it completely. Give him a treat as he shows curiosity about it. Let him step on it, but don't let him chew on it. Very slowly and gently touch him all over his body with the pole to desensitize him to it. Use your soft eyes and smile or even sing lightly to him as you pass the pole on his top line, down the back of his legs, up above his head, down the front of his legs, in-between his legs, behind his front legs, underneath his chest and in front of his back legs. Desensitizing can take a long time, or a very short time depending on how your dog responds to the pole. This period of desensitization can literally take weeks in some horses. The process is known as "sacking out" in horses, and is very helpful if that is done when the horse is very young. Their skin is very sensitive, being able to feel a fly alight anywhere on their body, and their instinctive nature gets set into motion to run away if they become frightened when touched unexpectedly with any object. Desensitization helps them to learn to overcome their instincts and to listen more to your direction.

After your dog is used to the pole, begin with the mount and dismount. While he is standing completely still, gently place the pole in the saddle. Make sure your dog does not move to try to brush the pole away. Then place the pole on top of the saddle and wiggle it lightly, making sure your dog stays still as he feels the movement and hears the sound. Do not bounce the pole in the saddle. Only adjust the weight lightly as if you were adjusting your seat or your stirrups in a saddle. Don't assume that since he accepts it all from one side that he will accept it all from the other. You must also repeat those movements from the other side of your dog just as with a horse.

Assuming your dog has allowed you to quietly place that pole on his back repeatedly, lunge him very slowly, letting him get used to the pole first at the walk, keeping the distance between you and your dog exactly equal, as that will help the pole stay on his back.

You can then progress to the trot and canter in both directions, but only progress if your dog is performing well in first the walk, then the trot, then the canter. Keep in mind that your reflexes should sharpen as well while holding that pole as still as you can (without pressing down on it) on the dog's back. When your dog moves faster than the walk, expect the pole to bounce. Just try to keep that pole very still. You will someday be doing the same thing without a pole but while riding a horse. It's up to you whether you let yourself ride like a pro, or like a sack of potatoes. The skill you develop in your hand/eye coordination in riding the dog will help in understanding the movement in riding a horse, and how you react to it.

Now you are ready to work in an arena. This is called flatwork. You will need a big, flat area like a yard, cleared of any debris such as toys, trash, sprinklers, hoses, etc. since you will be watching your dog while you are "riding" and not really looking where you are going. This, in fact, actually helps you to learn to separate the different movements in your body from his. That is, you will learn to maintain the same feeling, the same amount of a slight pull in your hand holding the rope to the dog, no matter if you are walking, standing still or running fast alongside your dog. This gives you a head start when it comes time to ride a horse. When riding a horse, good riders separate the movement of their hands from their seat and legs. Think of a jockey. His whole body is crouched down over the saddle. His stirrups are very, very short and he is actually squatting over a horse, not sitting on him. Watch racing horses closely. Imagine all that back and forth, up and down movement of the horse that the rider must not interfere with while riding. As the horse extends its neck and head out and in while galloping, the rider follows the horse's forward movement with his hands so he does not jerk the horse in the mouth. If the jockey kept his hands right on top of the horse's neck, or grabs the horse's mane while riding, this would jerk the horse in the mouth with every stride forward. His reins always remain at the very same length whether the horse's head is out or in. The jockey must not let his moving body parts interfere in any way with those of his moving horse. He must allow his body, his hands and his feet to move while following and not inhibiting the horse, but the movement in one does not affect the movement in another. That effect is what you should learn with your dog. If he moves forward, follow him with your hands, constantly feeling him at the end of your rope, but don't jerk him with the rope. Sensitize your hands to his movement. This is what is called "good, light hands" when riding a horse, something which is prized by horseback riders of every discipline.

When riding with a pole on your dog's back, you will need to change directions. Just as in lunging, ask your dog to "ho." Take the pole off of his back, put it in your hand which is holding the rope. Then take the rope from that one hand and put it in the other hand while keeping the pole in the first hand. Ask your dog to face you and then turn to the other direction. Put the pole back on your dog's back and resume your gaits.

If you had a broom, you could also be able to "post to the trot." Posting is something mostly English riders do, but I've seen Western riders do it as well. While riding a trotting horse, the rider will rise slightly upward from the saddle on every other beat, which in the long run is more comfortable for both horse and rider. Posting is only done at the trot, never at the walk or at the canter. To post properly, it is necessary that you understand the trot. The animal's legs move in a regular tempo, one-two-one-two-one-two. Watch how the dog's back will rise and fall, go up and down, up and down, up and down. Dogs trot much faster than a horse in tempo, so it's actually difficult to watch their legs closely, but their *diagonal (right front/left hind, left front/ right hind) legs* move alike. That means that when the front right leg moves forward, the hind left one also moves forward at the same time. While that is happening, the left front leg is moving back along with the right back leg. The process is repeated when the left front leg moves forward along with the right hind leg, and so on. You will also notice your little pole bouncing slightly on the dog's back, bounce-bounce-bounce. If you were to ride a horse at the trot, you would feel that bounce-bounce-bounce as the horse's movement moves you up and down in the saddle. It's an uncomfortable gait if you trot fast, so many people prefer to post to the trot. This means that with every other bounce, they stand up very slightly in their stirrups, up off of the saddle (not straight up but up, and forward into their thighs), and then sit back down in the middle (not the back of) saddle with the alternate bounce. Repeating that cycle, instead of feeling that bounce-bounce-bounce-bounce, posting lets you go up-down-up-down-up-down in the saddle voluntarily. It's the horse's movements that actually bounce you up, not your effort, so it's much more comfortable to ride that way and you still maintain control.

With your dog, you will first need to note the rhythm of their tempo at the trot. Notice how fast or slow your pole is naturally bouncing lightly on their back. Instead of just letting it sit there, try rolling the pole forward, then back, then forward, then back. This can actually be accomplished more easily with a broom: As you roll it forward toward the dog's shoulders, the back of the broom rises up off of the dog's back while the front of the broom stays sitting on the dog's shoulders. It's very similar to the way a rider's bottom moves in a saddle. When you get the hang of it, it's actually fun. But again, you should try to keep the movement minimal, only following the dog's natural bounce, without pushing him forward and without interfering with his movement in any way. Don't let the broom fall back with a bang onto the dog's back. This will help you understand that when you trot, you also should not just plop back down onto a horse's back, but land softly. Your horse will really appreciate that!

Equestrians are actually judged on how well they post the trot in horseshows.[15] The judge will notice if the rider is properly posting on the "correct diagonal" when a horse is trotting in an arena. (Don't confuse this with the "correct lead" which occurs only in the canter.) A rider is posting on the correct diagonal when they make their body rise up out of the saddle when the horse's "outside," front leg goes forward. This means that if your dog is in your arena, the outside leg is the front leg closest to the fence, not the one closest to you. For instance, if he is trotting around a circle to the left, his outside leg will be his right front leg. If you watch when that leg moves forward, you should have your pole or broom in the up or forward position in the saddle. When that leg moves back, bring your pole or broom back down into the resting position. With dogs, that happens very quickly like the ticking of a clock. Try to familiarize yourself with other breeds, large and small, and compare their tempos as they freely trot without a rider; watch the front, outer leg, and see how fast you would have to post to that trot. Then watch someone riding a horse English style. Watch how they rise and fall in the saddle at the trot while glancing down at the horses' legs. Put that trotting rhythm into your head. You have to be quick. Are they on the correct diagonal? They are if they are on the "outside diagonal."

The faster gait of the canter (or lope as it's called in western lingo) is almost like your dog is leaping forward in bunches of steps, just like a horse. The legs seem to move all at once, but unlike the trot, which is a two-beat gait with two legs hitting the ground at a time, the canter is a three-beat gait. When moving properly, the outside hind leg, the one closest to the outside fence, hits the ground first. That's the first beat. The second beat is actually when two hooves hit the ground at the same time, the inner hind leg and the outside front leg. The third and last beat at the canter is the front, inside leg. The leading, front leg is called the lead. They are either on the right or the left lead, but should always be on the "correct" lead. The horse is cantering on the inside (correct) lead if his inside front leg hits the ground last before taking that little leap with all of his feet off the ground. The inside lead could be left or right, depending on which way the horse is going, right or left in a circle. If circling to the left, the last hoof to hit the ground, making the third sound should be the inside or left foot, the left lead. The horse actually makes a very slight leap in-between each set of three beats, like someone drumming their fingers on a desk, 1-2-3 leap, 1-2-3 leap, 1-2-3 leap, etc.

People say the canter is usually more comfortable to ride than the trot, however, if the canter is not done properly, with the exact order of leg movement just described, a horse can be extremely uncomfortable to ride. They will also be off-balance and could slip and fall. You should watch that your dog's legs move on the correct lead in both directions. It gets tricky when you are moving in a straight line, and need to anticipate a turn to the right or left because you might have to change your lead. Equestrians are considered experts when they can actually make a horse canter on the correct lead, or change to the correct lead, anticipating a turn to either the right or the left which makes it easier for their horse to make a turn and not lose his balance. Try to study the canter. If this seems confusing at first, it is. Sorry about that. But with time, you will understand once your eyes become trained to follow the movement.

DRESSAGE

Dressage is simply the French word for *training*. It doesn't necessarily refer to English or Western training specifically, as "Western dressage" is now becoming more popular. What it does do is help any horse develop their potential properly and safely, starting with a solid foundation. It provides innumerable options for you to train your dog. In the very high levels of dressage, horses are seen to perform beautiful movements which, to the untrained eye, make the horse look like he is performing tricks. You should not even be able to see how the rider is asking his horse to move differently. That's the beauty of it all. It seems effortless. However, it can take years to properly bring a horse to the highest levels of dressage, and one should never resort to skipping any steps when training horses, or even dogs. Again, remember that your animal should always be physically ready to move up in training.

In dressage, patterns are ridden in a long, rectangular arena. The movements should be ridden in perfect circles, figure eights, perfectly straight lines, etc. There are letters regularly spaced around the arena exactly where movements are supposed to take place.

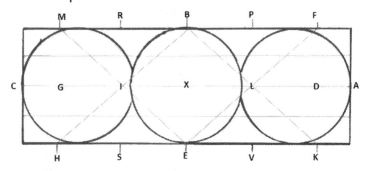

You can copy these letters and space them around your arena. Movements, such as the transition from walk to trot, should take place exactly at each letter. That means that your dog should walk up to the letter, but exactly when his shoulders (or the rider's body on a horse) pass that letter, the specific transition should be performed, such as moving from the walk to a trot. You should know how long it will take you to get your dog into a trot, just like it takes preparation to get a horse into a trot. Some horses need to be asked to trot two feet before the letter as they are very responsive, and some less attentive horses need 10 feet to be asked before they actually trot at that letter. It doesn't matter if your dog is responsive or not, it's completely up to you to know exactly what it will take to make your dog perform the trot at that letter. You must be the one in control and know exactly how soon before the letter to ask your dog for the desired movement.

The equestrian always tries to keep the horse's gaits pure and even in tempo -- not too fast nor too slow -- and with seamless transitions up or down. The transitions between the gaits should look effortless and smooth, not sudden or jarring. The circles performed should be perfectly round, not egg-shaped or square. The lines ridden along the long side of the arena, or on the diagonal from corner to corner should be straight, not wavy or zig-zag. There are many tests available at all levels through the United States Equestrian Federation, from Training Level through Prix St. Georges (pronounced Pree-Saint-George), which is the highest level attainable and the most difficult. Below is an example of one of the more simple tests in training level. The movements given are supposed to be performed at each of the different letters.

Some tips are added for each movement that help to perform the movement properly.

At A, Enter working trot

Tip: Straightness on centerline and in halt; immobility; quality of trot; willing, balanced transitions.

At X, Halt, Salute. Proceed at working trot (a good, steady tempo, not lazy).

At C, Track left. Bend and balance in turn.

Tip: Quality of trot; shape and size of circle; bend.

At E, Circle left (20-meter diameter circle)

At A, Circle left (20-meter diameter circle). Developing left lead canter second half of circle.

Tip: Quality of trot and canter; willing, calm transition; shape and size of circle; bend.

Straight line through AFB, Working canter.

From B-E, Half circle left (20-meter diameter half circle)

Tip: Quality of canter; shape and size of half circle; bend.

Between E & K, Working trot.

Tip: Willing, balanced transition; quality of canter and trot.

At A, Circle left (20-meter diameter circle).

Tip: Rising trot, allowing the horse to stretch forward and downward. Stretch over the back into a light contact maintaining balance and quality of trot; bend; shape and size of circle; smooth, balanced transitions.

Before A, Shorten the reins.

At A, Working trot.

Between A & F, Medium walk.

Tip: Willing, balanced transition; quality of trot and walk.

Through F-X-H, Free walk.

Tip: Reach and ground cover of free walk allowing complete freedom to stretch the neck forward and downward; quality and regularity of medium walk; willing, balanced transitions; straightness on diagonal. This exercise proves that your animal is soft and relaxed – any nervousness will show itself in his back and neck.

From H-C, Medium walk.

At C, Working trot.

Tip: Willing, balanced transition; quality of trot.

At B, Circle right (20-meter diameter circle)

Tip: Quality of trot; shape and size of circle; bend.

At A, Circle right (20-meter diameter circle), developing right lead canter second half of circle.

Tip: Quality of trot and canter; willing, calm transition; shape and size of circle; bend.

From A-K-E, Working canter.

From E-B, Half circle right (20-meter diameter circle).

Tip: Quality of canter; shape and size of half circle; bend.

Between B & F, Working trot.

Tip: Willing, balanced transition; quality of canter and trot.

At A, Down centerline.

Tip: Bend and balance in turn; straightness on centerline and in halt; willing, balanced transition; immobility.

At X, Halt and salute.

You can find more tests like these online at the USEF website, www.usef.org. You could also search the Internet for videos that show dressage riders riding a test to see how long it takes, how the horse looks, if he is performing movements exactly at the letters, as well as what the rider is actually doing while riding his horse.

JUMPING

One of the first things that comes to mind for many people when they think of horses is the beautiful image of a horse sailing over a jump. Dogs can do that, too, but obviously not at the same height as a horse. This is an area where many dogs excel. It has been called agility and is sanctioned by the American Kennel Club. There are trials where dogs compete against each other. They are judged by how precisely they navigate and jump a course, as well as the time it takes them to complete it. I do not aim to cover agility trials here, but will attempt to show you how dogs are very similar to horses in how they jump.

A horse will successfully jump an obstacle completely. They must clear the jump without knocking it over or even touching it with their feet. Dogs on the other hand will often choose to jump on top of an obstacle and then jump down from it. If you want to train your dog to clear a jump successfully like a horse, he should learn to sail over the jump by himself (without any help from you on the other end of the rope) and recover on all four feet, that is not fall over, on the other side.

There are several kinds of jumps. Cavaletti are poles evenly spaced apart, lying flat on the ground, or just slightly elevated. These jumps are meant to gauge the tempo of a horse's gait. They help teach the horse to carefully pick up his feet and not walk on top of the poles but successfully place all four feet evenly between the series of poles. Another kind of jump is called the cross rails. These are two poles held up on opposite ends to form a cross or X in the middle (see photo). The side columns that hold them up are called standards, and the pole height can be adjusted up or down on the standards with cups. When the poles are elevated from one side standard to the other horizontally straight across, it's called a vertical jump. Again, the height is adjustable. When two vertical jumps are lined up, one in front of the other 1-2 feet apart, it's called an oxer. When there is a deep and wide hole in the ground, it's called a ditch, and when that hole is filled with water, it's called a water obstacle, tray or stream.

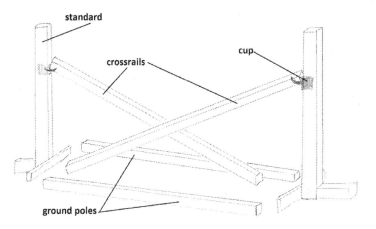

There are five segments to a jump: Approach, take-off, flight, landing and departure.

Approach: It's up to you to make sure your dog's approach to any obstacle is very, very straight, perfectly perpendicular many feet before the actual obstacle. If you let your dog approach at an angle from the side, you are making it more difficult for him to jump the obstacle properly, plus you are making it much easier for him to refuse. If you were riding a horse and your horse refused a jump, you could very likely fly over the jump without the horse, which I'm sure you know would hurt! If you approach an obstacle perpendicularly and right at the middle of the jump, you increase your chances of your dog successfully clearing that jump. A perfect approach is the best foundation for a successful jump, and it's completely up to you to set it up correctly. Learn the evasions your dog might take. Does he choose to refuse the jump and run out to the right? Next time be ready to keep him on course with a better hold of your rope (again, not pulling, just feeling him at the end of it).

Does your dog often stop right in front of the jump? Maybe you need to learn how fast he needs to be going to clear it properly. You must be aware of how fast your dog needs to be going to clear a jump. Obviously, they don't need to be going very fast over a low jump, like a tree branch lying on the ground, and in fact your dog could step over that branch at a walk. However, if he's going too slowly, he might also think he could step up on top of the branch then step down. Horses generally don't have the choice of actually jumping up onto a jump, unless they are jumping an obstacle called a bank jump, which is a huge mound of dirt with a sudden elevation where a horse actually jumps up on top of the bank, and then jumps down off of it. Most jumps are not like that. You must also give your dog enough distance before the obstacle to jump so that he can get up enough speed should he need it to clear the jump successfully. There are many things to consider in the approach of a jump to allow your dog to clear it successfully. You must learn all that it takes to get your dog approaching in the best possible way.

Take-off and flight: Horses that are natural-born jumpers seem to know the exact speed and distance it would take to jump an obstacle. Some horses are so full of steam that they always go too fast, not having enough time to set themselves up correctly, to bring their hind legs underneath and elevate their front end. This could mean disaster if they knocked over a fence. It's only the truly skilled equestrians who can ride those "hot" horses. A very skilled rider can actually help their horse take off right at the exact spot they should in order to clear a fence successfully. You will gain that knowledge by only starting out with the very lowest fences and note where the dog needs to take off as you increase the size of the jumps. PLEASE do not ask your dog to jump a large obstacle at first. Their bodies also need to build up naturally to be able to have the physical capacity and mental confidence to safely jump larger obstacles. The flight will only last a second or two. Do not interfere with your dog's movement at all during this time. As well, watch what happens to your lunge rope when your dog jumps over any obstacle. Make absolutely certain that the rope does not get caught by the standards on the side or a corner of the jump. That would severely unbalance your dog in flight and he might not land safely. You can let the rope out a little or flip it over the standard or side of a jump so that it quietly follows your dog, but do remember to not "help" your dog over the jump by pulling on the rope.

Landing: When your dog lands after a jump, he'll be using his two front legs, then his two hind legs. You should allow him to balance himself. If your dog happens to have knocked the jump down, you need to be there to help him get out of the way, so just be ready. Always keep your primary visual focus on your dog but keep his surroundings softly in view as well.

Departure: Assuming he has landed the proper way, allow your dog to keep going in a straight line, and then bring him back down to a halt. You could praise him at this time; just make sure he stays still. Keep him stopped for a few seconds to regain his composure. It's a very, very exciting thing to watch a dog jump, and dogs often get carried away, but if your dog gets too excited, you will lose control of him. You will need to work that straight line back down to a halt for awhile before progressing onto a series of jumps in an arena.

When placing cavaletti, you'll need to measure how long your dog's stride is. You'll also need poles, preferably at least 4, but up to 8 is better. Eight-foot-long PVC poles used for irrigation can be bought at a hardware store. If you use this length of pole, you'll also be able to use them for building jumps. You could get by with the smallest diameter of PVC poles, $\frac{1}{2}$ inch, but some bigger dogs might not respect that size, and might step on them instead of over them. However, $\frac{1}{2}$-inch poles will bend too much if you used them elevated as cross rails. On the other hand, 4-inch-diameter poles are just too big for the legs of a small dog like a Yorkie even when placed low on the ground, so your best bet is to buy 1/2-inch poles for the smaller breeds.

At first, only ask your dog to trot over a single pole laid flat on the ground. Make sure he does step over, not on top of it. Do not place any more poles down until you are sure of the length of your dog's stride. To measure the stride of your dog at the trot, you'll need to trot him along and watch his inside front leg. It's good to do this in sand as he will leave a mark with that paw in the sand. When he trots, the next spot where he places his paw will be the second point. Measure in-between the two paw prints and that's the length of his natural stride at the trot. That's the distance you will place between the cavaletti at first. Trot him over the cavaletti poles many times in both directions. He should be trotting over the poles without stepping on them so as not to disturb the placement of the poles. If he happens to step on a pole, displacing it, stop your dog to replace the pole. DO NOT let him keep trotting over the poles if they are uneven.

The beauty of the cavaletti comes when you lengthen the space between the poles. You will then begin to develop your dog's stride. This becomes a great exercise for him. Only increase the length between the poles an inch at a time and make sure your dog is very comfortable with trotting evenly over those poles, that is keeps an even rhythm with one step in-between poles. Watch the beauty of your dog as he increases the length of his stride. It looks like they will be trotting in slower motion, higher up and longer in stride. This is excellent for the development of their joints and muscles. Do not be discouraged, however, if your dog just doesn't understand how to navigate his stride evenly over the poles. You will see if the poles are set too far apart, as he could step twice in-between poles, which defeats the purpose.

Once your pet has perfectly mastered the cavaletti, you may begin to raise the height of the jump. Standards, the two wooden structures on the sides of the jumps, are built from sturdy wood, 4x4 in diameter, and several feet tall. There are holes spaced 3 inches apart where cups are placed to hold the poles. The holes allow the poles to be raised or lowered. You won't need to go out and buy wood to build the standards, as you could use pretty much anything you have on hand around the house or yard that would safely hold up the poles on the sides of a jump, like short chairs laid on their side, cinder blocks, or even your friends (if you trust they won't drop the poles or raise them without warning). Please be careful in what you choose to use as a jump obstacle. Be sure that it has no sharp edges that can cut your dog if he landed on it or passed by it, no protruding nails that he could puncture himself, and nothing that could trap or bruise him if it landed on him.

It would be safest in the beginning to use the cross-pole jump. That looks like a big X, with the lowest part being right in the middle. This will also encourage your dog to always jump right in the middle. Sometimes just using two poles to make an X can confuse a dog as it's more difficult to gauge how tall that jump is, so some people put ground poles right in front of the jump on the ground, and right behind the jump just so the animal can negotiate it better. The span from the front of the jump to the back of the jump is only a few inches if you do it this way. You can also place yet another pole a few strides in front of the jump. Then the dog has to clear that pole on the ground, and then still jump that second cross-pole jump. This combination of jumps is called an in-and-out. You can set up an obstacle course for your dog, but always, always keep in mind the five components to jumping, approach, take-off, flight, landing and departure. You should completely focus on your dog during all five movements in order to maintain his trust and his safety. Do not take any shortcuts with any of the movements.

When you start increasing the height and span of your jumps, you will have to increase the speed of your dog's gait somewhat. You will develop your dog properly and safely if you start out with low jumps. Only then should you increase the size of the jump. There will come the time, however, when your dog will reach his limit in the size of a jump. Don't be discouraged.[16] You might try setting up a course of jumps, each one different, each spaced differently, so that you could do several combinations of jumps. You will soon learn what your dog is capable of jumping, how high, how wide, and how much distance he needs in his approach to clear a fence. Use that as a gauge to set up your combination. With my Bambi, I used a low beachchair as an oxer, two patio chairs turned on their sides as an in-and-out, the wooden picnic bench seats first as a one-stride then two-stride in-and-out, and my mother's gardening buckets set next to each other, bottom-to-bottom, as a barrel-type jump. There are many Internet websites with combinations of different types of jumps to give you some ideas, as in cross country or stadium jumping, that you could use to practice your learned expertise. Plus, there are always other areas to have fun with your dog, like Western style.

WESTERN

In horseback riding, the biggest difference you'll notice between English and Western riding is the saddle. In fact, the Western saddle is usually a lot bigger and a lot heavier than an English saddle. It also generally has a horn, that thing that looks like a handle that beginning riders usually like to hold onto. In reality, that horn was developed to help tie up and hold a calf out on the range. When you start riding, you will impress your riding instructor if you DO NOT hold onto that horn. It's the sign of a rank beginner. Western riding, however, in my opinion is much safer for the rider than English because the saddle is bigger and seems more stable. When I used to teach riding, I always started beginners out in a Western saddle, just in case they needed that horn to hold onto at the last minute to maintain their balance, and to readjust where they needed to be -- that is, right in the middle of the seat. Balance, yours and the horse's, is probably the most important thing in horseback riding. Without balance, you'll fall off. Holding on helps you stay in the middle by providing you that central part with which to base your body. But don't keep holding onto that horn. Balance should be maintained with legs held relaxed and long, down and around the horse's body. It is not that you'll need that in training your dog, but I'd like you to remember that one tip when you do eventually start riding horses.

Western riding includes many ways of enjoying your horse, and dog. There is barrel racing, trail riding, team penning, cutting, reining, gymkhana and roping. Of course, you won't be able to do team penning or roping off of your dog as those sports require the use of cows. Dogs just aren't large enough to run alongside a cow, let alone hold a tied cow still, although some breeds like the Australian Shepherd work with sheep. That's not quite the same as using your dog as a horse in this book. Your dog can, however, be taught how to race around barrels, perform "reining" maneuvers, and go trail riding.

Barrel racing requires a very energetic dog, as it's based on who in a team can run around three barrels the fastest without knocking any of the barrels down. It's generally a team event involving several participants, but you can see how much your dog will improve in his time with your training. For your dog, you could use trashcans from your home as the barrels.

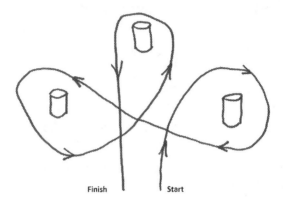

Finish   Start

According to the picture above, you will place three barrels or cans at the same distance from each other in three corners of your arena. The bottom of the square is the point where you start and finish. You will probably need someone to time you at first, just to let you see how much you have improved.

The clock begins when your dog passes over the starting line. He'll first run to the first barrel on his right hand side, turn around clockwise all the way around the barrel. Then he'll race to the second barrel and turn around it but now counter-clockwise, to the left, and the third barrel should be raced around to the left again. After the third barrel, the race is on to get to that finish line as fast as possible.

The event is based on time, but you can get disqualified. The faster you finish without being disqualified, the better. If you turn in the wrong direction, you are disqualified. If you knock a barrel down, you are disqualified. You'll have to figure out at this point what made your dog knock a barrel down. Was he too close? Did your rope catch a barrel? Was he going too fast? Did his flopping, flying ears knock the barrel down? Did he stop to pee on a barrel? (Sorry, couldn't resist that one.)

When your dog gets used to the pattern, you won't have to run right alongside him and to the outside of the barrels, but let him do most of the work. When you come to the first barrel, stop in front of it and ask your dog to go around the barrel by himself in the appropriate direction, using your right arm. All you need to do is point with the hand holding the rope. You can verbally ask your dog to "go around," or "go on" or just "barrel" or "take it." Just make sure whatever command you use to ask him with one barrel, you will use the exact same words and tone of voice with the other barrels. That's how he'll learn and take less time. Make sure you allow enough slack in the rope to let it travel around with him, and don't let the rope touch the barrel or you'll knock it over (losing the race for your dog!). It might take some practice in letting out the slack in the rope and then taking it up again. This is good practice for when you start riding when you need to give your horse some more length in your reins.

REINING

Reining is the Western version of English dressage. It contains more dramatic movements than dressage, which should be mentioned here. Reining was developed to show the different movements in ranch horses that were needed to sort cows on the old range. These movements are performed in an arena. The horse performs small, controlled circles, large, fast circles, flying "lead" changes, rollbacks over the hind end, full, complete spins performed in place and sliding stops. All of these movements, like dressage, should be gradually taught to your dog so he does not injure himself. I would not suggest doing sliding stops on a young puppy as that could damage his growing bones. The quick, jarring movements should wait until your dog's skeletal system is fully formed, preferably after he is at least a year of age.

Once again, your dog should be trained to move at any gait on the leash. If you do find a miniature western saddle for him to wear, keep in mind that it might flop around a bit more than an English one, so make sure your straps fit him well without being too tight. Some Western saddles have a rear cinch that is not tightened, but kept loose. Its sole purpose is to keep the back of the saddle from flopping around too much, but in male dogs, that cinch might interfere with the dog's private gear. Therefore, make sure it's loose enough so it doesn't hurt him down there, but still long enough so that his hind legs can't walk into those straps. Also, in Western style, horses wear "skid boots" to protect their hocks, the back joint of their leg that can hit and scrape the ground when doing sliding stops. I wouldn't recommend that you put these on your dog unless you are only working on gravel, as dogs' hair is usually a bit thicker than horses'. When starting out in reining, do the movements slowly at first to make sure your dog is performing a perfectly formed circle, not a square, then speed them up.

Performing a flying lead change will probably be very difficult for your dog to perform. The term, "lead" is only used when referring to the canter or lope (the Western word for canter). To refresh your memory of the sequence of footfalls during each gait, refer to the chapter "Disciplines," where the gaits are described. You will know if your dog is on the correct lead if his front, inside foot (the one closest to you) hits the ground last. If you are circling your dog around to the left, his left front foot should be the last of all of his feet to hit the ground before he takes that little leap and another stride. If his outer, right foot hits the ground last, he is not on the correct lead, and he is not optimally balanced while moving to the left, and vice versa to the right.

Dogs often change their leads at will when loping around. Generally, it's instinctive for them to change to their "left lead" when turning to the left, and "right lead when turning to the right. When going in a straight line, however, how can you make your dog change his lead on command? It's not easy. Just as it takes years for a horse to learn to do that on command, it will also take a long time for your dog to learn to change leads. When you are riding a horse, you have many more aids -- your legs, seat balance, reins -- to help you signal to the horse that you want him to change his leads. In fact, not many horses can change their leads within a single stride. Most need to learn to do this by loping, then coming down to a trot, and then changing their lead to the other direction. In time, they learn to automatically change their leads within the canter.

To help you perform a lead change, work your dog in a large figure-of-eight pattern. Get him used to trotting in a figure-of-eight pattern first before asking for the canter. Turn your dog in a complete circle to the right and then just before coming to the middle of the 8, bring him down to a trot and then send him off to the left at a canter. Hopefully, he'll realize that he needs to change to the left lead to stay in balance. With your dog, it will be a matter of luck whether or not he gets the hang of changing his lead by your command alone. Chances are it won't happen, but consider yourself lucky if it does. A flying lead change in a dog should not be scored too heavily for this reason.

TRAIL RIDING

If you like taking your dog for a walk, this should be a breeze. Each time you go outside for fun with your dog, you are actually going trail riding. However, with horses, this can be a time to let your hair down. Some trail riding functions are seriously judged at special shows. Trail riding events can be done in arenas using things that you normally find on trails, like small logs to jump, gaits to open, flapping flags and other scary objects such as those found on a trail, just to see how your dog reacts to them. A perfect trail horse will do whatever its rider asks without endangering itself or its rider by running away from fear, rearing, or even refusing to go forward after being asked. That's what's called a "bombproof horse." You should familiarize your dog with some of these things. Fortunately, if a dog shies away from an object, you will not be hurt, unlike a green (young and untrained) horse on a trail who can so suddenly jump to the side that you would lose your balance in the saddle, or worse. Since horses often listen more to their instinct than what their rider is telling them, horses often get skittish, turn around very quickly and run away. This is another reason to always maintain the best balance while in the saddle. This can actually happen anywhere while riding if something unexpected comes into the horse's view. That is why it's up to you to anticipate being able to handle anything that can come your way and never take chances on a horse. Never ride a horse that you know is beyond your experience of riding. They are always bigger than you are. And do try to go trail riding with others, not alone, for safety. Even then when riding horses, please wear a helmet.

One of a few things you may encounter on the trail is a log lying in your path. You could either go around it, or jump it. If you followed the instructions in the jumping section of this book, jumping that log should be no problem, and jumping a ditch should be no problem. What if you come to a hill? With horses, it is much safer to remain at a walk when both going up as well as descending a hill. If you let your horse trot up or down as is their nature to do, it could lose its balance because of the way its weight is distributed, especially when going downhill. If a big horse falls on its knees, not only will you definitely be thrown off, but that horse could injure himself severely as well, and any bad injury of a horse's legs could mean the end of your horse's career. Please don't take chances with horses or dogs. Learn to ride safely from the beginning and you should have no regrets.

What if you come to a closed gate on a trail? If it's locked, you are not supposed to go through under any circumstance (unless you have the key with permission to use it). Trespassing onto private property is illegal. But if that gait is simply closed, not locked, and if you were riding a horse, you might have to open it while you are still in the saddle. If you have worked with your dog, following the instructions in this book, you should have the manual dexterity and coordination necessary to be able to handle moving your horse around while opening that gate. While working with your dog, you should learn the basics of opening a gate with your dog in hand. Bring your dog off to the side of the gate. First have him stand out of the way of the swinging gate, and then have him move closely next to you as you push the gate open. Do not let your dog or horse ever take the lead going through a door while leading them. I would encourage you to walk through the gate first, and allow your dog to follow but closely.[17] You would be doing the same thing if you were riding a horse. Closing the gate is a bit more difficult. You need to get close enough to the handle of the gate, then step your dog backwards (slowly saying "back, back") or sideways (saying "over, over") away from the moving gate, slowly as you pull it shut. That's how it is done in the trail riding events. You are not allowed to dismount, open and close the gate and then get back on your horse as that would be cheating. Wouldn't you rather be a Master Canine Equestrian? You will be well on your way after reading this book!

DRIVING

In equestrian terms, driving is when a horse wears a harness and pulls something behind him like a cart, carriage, buggy, wagon or plow. The driver is the person sitting in the cart, controlling the horse through the reins usually behind the horse, but sometimes to its side. There are different kinds of driving, like when a horse pulls a plow on a farm, actually pulling a wagon, and when a young horse is in his early stages of training with ground driving where the horse only wears a harness and doesn't really pull anything. I personally love to always teach my young horses to ground drive. The young horse must already be familiar with turning to the right and left, as well as wearing either a saddle or harness on his body. It's perfect for the horse who isn't quite ready to handle a rider in his back in the saddle. It also allows me to follow the horse from behind him as he moves forward, which is indispensible in safely learning how a horse will handle sights on the trail that could otherwise spook a young horse. Since I'm not riding him, I can't fall off, but can learn what it would take to bring the horse back under control, giving me a safe head start for when the time comes to ride him. It can also safely give a horse experience out on the trail who isn't otherwise quiet enough or old enough to handle a rider.

When a horse is up at the front by himself with no one at either side of him to be able to turn to should a scary situation arise, a horse must learn to think for himself. He must have enough confidence to make his own, rational decisions, and to also learn to quietly accept direction from the driver who is usually behind him. This can take time as not all horses are leaders. Some would rather let another horse blaze the trail in front of him so he wouldn't have to see things first and make the big decisions. That's yet another reason why you must maintain the trust and respect your horse and dog have in you. He must know to depend on you to give him the answer to any question he has to any challenge he faces.

Dogs have long been known to have the capacity to pull things. The Iditarod is the race in Alaska where teams of dogs pull a man in his sled over snowy grounds. In another event, some bigger, muscular dogs are put in contests to see how much weight they can pull. Any dog must have the power to pull the weight that they are being asked to pull or else they can hurt themselves. This is where your breed will decide what sort of things your dog can pull. A Chihuahua will not be able to pull much more than a small toy cart, whereas a St. Bernard can likely pull a very small child in a little red wagon.

When I was a kid, I had a myriad of toy contraptions that were made for toy horses. My poodle, Bambi, weighed only 10 pounds, so I couldn't ask him to pull much more than a pound or two if it had wheels. My favorite vehicle was a wooden Old West wagon made out of lightweight pine wood. It had four wheels, a box in the middle, a removable "bonnet" to cover the cargo and a double tree for the front, meaning it was meant for two toy horses. Bambi was my only dog so I changed the double tree of the wagon into a single tree, meaning there were two shafts sticking out to put on both sides of his body. Each shaft was attached to the axel of one of the front wheels so that when Bambi turned to the right or left, the shafts which were attached to him made the wheels follow his body and turn with him. I put lightweight things inside that wagon, like my Barbie dolls, my hamster (in a tiny cage so he wouldn't jump out), and flowers. You can even see little dogs in parades these days, dressed up fancifully, pulling tiny wagons made for them. They love to get the crowd's attention.

In the olden days (actually way before I was born), horses used to pull carriages to help deliver things like milk and ice to family homes. In the big cities like New York, when the gasoline-powered automobile started replacing horse-drawn carriages, delivery companies actually preferred to keep their horses and carts rather than change over to any gasoline truck. Horse-drawn vehicles were preferred because the horses actually knew their routes, saving the driver time. As the driver prepared his goods for each address in his wagon, the horse would automatically go to the next address where the driver would simply drop off the products, letting the horse do his thing. At the time this book was written, New York City still had horse-drawn carriage rides which wind through Central Park, giving residents and visitors alike a taste of what it was like to live in a city where the only means of transportation was with horses. Passengers get to feel what it is like to travel in a much slower and relaxing pace than that felt in a car. They hear the clippity-clop of the horse's hooves on the pavement. Taking a ride in a carriage is a romantic visit to our historic times, when horses literally helped build the country. Driving horses is a sport still practiced in this country for the select few. But if you have a dog, you can make it happen.

I taught Bambi to ground drive first, before I actually hitched him to anything. He already knew the voice commands for walk and trot. He didn't perform the canter well when I was behind him with the reins, plus I didn't like to keep running after him. I was afraid I wouldn't have enough warning in case he stopped and I might step on him, so we just walked and trotted while ground-driving.

Your dog should be able to stop and stand without moving until you ask him to move forward. This is for safety reasons. You'll need him to stand still while you attach his pulling harness and the cart or whatever you intend for him to pull. To see if he is able to do this, test him by asking him to halt. While looking at him (a sign of dominance to him which helps him to obey), ask him to "stay" and take one step to his side. If he also takes a step, gently ask him to come to a halt again and say "stay." Take another step and see if he realizes he should stay until you ask him to move. You may need to repeat the process of asking him to halt and stay several times until he understands perfectly.

When he does stay put, try taking two steps, then three, etc. until you can actually walk all the way around him in a circle as he stands (not even sits) completely still. This could take some time, but again, it's important to teach your dog to stay put before teaching him to drive. The reason for this is for when it comes time to attach his harness and cart. It just wouldn't do if he moved around when that was performed.

Since dogs do not use a bit in their mouths and a bridle around their heads, it is at this time that you could start using a collar instead of the regular harness you've been using up until now. It is easier for your dog to feel your turning signals when you are out of his sight when the collar is on his neck rather than trying to turn him through the harness. Using a collar to turn your dog should not interfere with the movement of the harness when they are worn together. The collar should be one that has two attachments, such as O rings or D rings, to attach the left rein on the left side of the collar, and another attachment on the right side of the collar.

Attach one side of your rope to the left-sided attachment only. Keep your dog facing forward, but take a few steps away from your dog's left side while you are facing him. Speaking the word "Haw" means turn left to sled dogs as well as horses that pull heavy weight in agriculture, so you could start using this word to turn left. Pull on the left-sided rein very gently while saying "Haw" until your dog turns to you and walks up to you. Switch your rope to the right side and do the same on that side but when turning to the right say "Gee" (pronounced "jee"). Try to feel how much pressure it takes to turn your dog. Never just pull his body to you without letting him step–toward you willingly. It should only take very minimal pressure. Practice this exercise with only the smallest amount of pressure possible so he does not become desensitized to turning. Eventually he will need to respond to your asking him to turn while you are saying Haw and Gee without having to actually feel the pull.

You will need to fit your dog with a special cart harness that he will wear comfortably while pulling the cart. I don't suggest that you use the same harness that you have been using up until this time as it will not work as well as a harness used to pull. There are special harnesses you could buy made out of nylon that are made for dogs who pull sleds. These harnesses have various shapes, some look like an H from the top, some look like the letter Y, and some look like the letter, X. But for horses, the harnesses are of two types. The Dutch collar (first picture below) has a thick chest strap that passes around the front of the horses' chest, just below the lowest part of his neck. Then there is a Hames collar (second picture below) which is made from what looks like two curved, rigid sticks which are very padded. When this is positioned around the bottom of a horses' neck, it distributes the weight that the horse is pulling. Dogs don't wear the Hames-type collar, only the Dutch style due to the differences in their conformation to a horse.

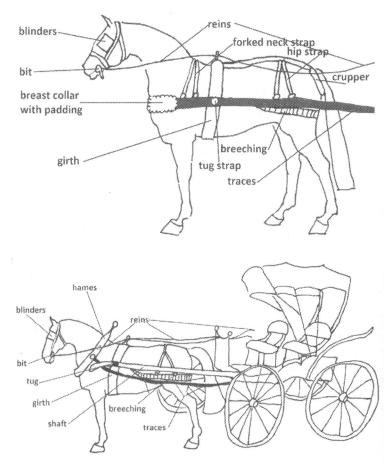

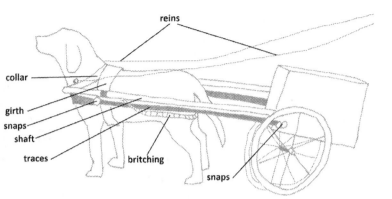

If you can't buy a harness that looks like an H harness, you can make one. When I was a kid, I used one-inch-wide grosgrain ribbon to go around Bambi's ribcage and front of his shoulders. This laid flat and did not rub into his skin like string or rope would. You can also buy nylon webbing at a hardware store if you have a bigger dog. Ribbon or webbing can be sewn or knotted together to look like horse harness. The chest strap across your dog's chest should be pretty wide as this is the part that will mainly be pressing against him when he pulls. You could also either tie loops in the ribbon, or attach O rings similar to those used for key rings. Separate it slightly and slide the point of one end into the ribbon or strap, then keep turning the O ring around until it has attached to the strap, as if you were adding a key. You will attach the cart's traces to the O rings.

You can attach ropes to his harness, but be careful they aren't too short or his hind legs will hit what he is pulling. However, if the lines are too long, he could get the lines caught around his feet. They also need to be high enough off the ground so that he can't get those lines caught between his hind legs. If you use a cart with two shafts, they will need to be placed one on each side of your dog's body. The function of shafts not only help the cart follow the forward movement of the dog, but they follow his turning as well as push the cart backwards when your dog backs up. If you only had ropes attaching your dog to a cart, your dog would only be able to pull it forward, not backward as the ropes would collapse. The ends of the shafts should be long enough to reach the front of his shoulder. If they are too short, they could poke him in his side when he turns. Your ropes must also be attached securely to those shafts so that the dog won't leave that cart behind!

If you don't have a cart, your dog can pull other things, such as a skateboard, or things without wheels, but just make sure they aren't too heavy. Try having him drag an empty backpack or an empty box. Just remember, never have your dog pull your own weight. That is, don't stand on your skateboard or sit in that box. Keep in mind that it takes many dogs to even pull a dog sled in the snow in Alaska.

After your dog masters pulling that cart, you could either lead him at his left side, or ground drive him wherever you want. You could use him to help collect fruit in your yard, gather pinecones in a forest, or maybe save you a couple of trips to the car when you bring in the groceries. Dogs just love to have a job, and they'll love you more for showing them how to be a part of your life!

Afterword

Hopefully, after reading this book, you have learned how similar your dog and a horse are. You have learned what you can and can't do with a dog to turn him into a horse as closely and safely as possible. The techniques in this book can be your stepping stone to try other equestrian disciplines with your dog. May I suggest getting your friends together who have dogs and having a fun canine equestrian show with a judge, and maybe even a cameraman to capture the event? You will find that the more you practice, the more you can achieve with your dog, and ultimately you will love your dog even more as a working partner. Having a friendly, competitive neighborhood show could push you past your own boundaries that you thought insurmountable, and you will be able to compare your work against that of other human/canine partners. Learning camaraderie is ideal, and will help you if you eventually decide to compete on your horse. It will also be more fulfilling to know that you helped to train your horse by learning some techniques with your dog. That always feels better than just buying an expensive horse that has already been trained. Working with your dog, or your horse, makes your partner a bigger part of you.

Once you truly master all the techniques of this book, you will be able to judge the differences among other dogs and the partnership with their trainers. This will eventually qualify you to be a respected judge. Only through the process of learning a task and comparing yourself to others in the same role will you learn your and your dog's strengths and deficiencies. It's only by learning these that you can improve your and your dog's circumstances, and become a proven professional in the field of working with animals. More specifically, you will soon develop a better understanding of watching people ride and learn even more about the wonderful world of horses. I've loved dogs and horses all of my life and seem to still learn something new every day.

The lessons in this book are a wonderful option for you to expand your relationship with your dog, and your own horse someday. Here are the means of bringing your love and understanding of your dog to a whole new level, one that can encompass as much as you want it to in simple theory alone, in the promotion of wellness in you and your dog, and ultimately in expanding your dream of horsemanship.

Endnotes

1   It must be in the genes. Many people are born
    loving horses and I certainly was one of them.
    I was born in middle-class suburbia, not in the
    country. No one else in my family carries the
    trait so maybe the gene just sprouted in me
    when I was born. Though my brother and I were
    raised the same way, he is completely devoid
    of the animal-crazy gene. In fact, it took him
    50 years to finally learn, only out of necessity,
    how to gingerly pet a dog, and only due to the
    patient instruction of his animal-loving wife and
    daughters.

2   My earliest childhood memories are from a TV
    show in 1960s Philadelphia hosted by a cowgirl
    with bling, Sally Starr. In the beginning of
    every show, in all of her fancy Western wear
    and fringe, Sally gallops her bodacious Palomino
    across an open field. In my mind I galloped my
    horse alongside in wanton abandon. This led me
    to act out my dreams with my toys, which were,
    of course, mostly horses. Whenever entering
    a toy store, I first looked for the horses.
    Eventually, horse-related toys made up most of
    my collection. I was thrilled when dolls were
    made with hinged appendages as they could ride

atop my horses. My favorite toys were the Marx Johnny West figures and horses. They were practically unbreakable and suited my needs quite well for many years. But even Barbies would do, as long as they were bendable. My horses galloped all over the house. I used to also run the garden hose in the backyard at a trickle in order to simulate a running stream for my horses to drink from, and I built a stable yard around it. I used long strands of grass tied around sticks to build my stalls and arena, then filled it all in with my little toy horses, riders and barnyard animals, just like a riding stable, or what I imagined one to be like. My dreamy outdoor setup lasted for days until the next rainstorm washed it all away. Then I would just build another one, which was usually completely different. Sometimes I had a hunter/jumper stable, sometimes it was western-themed for barrel racing, and sometimes it was my own personal dream stable that I would certainly live above some day.

3 Parents use a few feeble reasons with their children about why they need to remain horseless. Every horse-crazy person has heard it all before. "What do you need a horse for?" "Horses aren't for everyone." "We can't afford one." "They are expensive to buy and even more expensive to keep." "They aren't for the faint of heart, the very young or very unfit unless fully

trained which, of course, increases their price exponentially." I often laugh at a parent who wants to find that "bombproof" (safe), beautiful pony for their kid to plop around on – "for cheap." The hard reality is that it costs several thousand dollars to buy a trustworthy horse, and hundreds more each month for boarding, lessons, a bridle and saddle, vaccinations, veterinarian fees, etc. plus multiple, unexpected odds and ends. Learning how to ride or even handle a horse is time-consuming, expensive and possibly dangerous. Horses also need to live where it is legal to keep them, making access practically impossible for most people in cities or suburbs. Unfortunately, all the seemingly rational reasons are simply no argument when someone, child or adult, has the horse-crazy gene. The excuses fall on deaf ears.

4   The most frustrating side of my childhood story was my memory of begging my parents for a horse. They fought back with all they could muster because parents are Supposed to be more clever. I remember the first time I heard my father say "Sure, we could afford the horse." He waited for my exhilaration. Then came the punch line. "It's the upkeep we can't afford," he added, quite pleased with his sharp wit. He then explained that we barely had 1/4 acre in suburbia, and knew I would appreciate the fact that neighborhood zoning laws did not

allow animals of that size to live in a backyard. But, dad, I already had our whole yard planned out. The arena would go around the apple tree, toward the sycamore, up past the plum trees and back around. The horse could live in our garage. What's the big deal? Zoning, schmoning. I still had that lingering feeling of being deprived. I Needed a horse. It had become my mission in life.

5   I managed to fit horses into my otherwise non-horsey life. When one is a motivated, young adult, free from the encumbrances of family life, one can choose to live in areas close to riding facilities. I once lived in New York City where only the lucky few owned a car, the only real option to commute to any horse community away from the city. I learned to happily suffer the hour it took to ride the subway, and then to take a 20-minute (expensive) taxi ride, proudly wearing my tweed jacket, my tall, black boots and with my hardhat under my arm during the long trip to the stable in Jamaica Bay, where my trusty steed awaited. I half-leased her to ride her one day a weekend. To pay for her, I provided riding lessons in Prospect Park the other day of the weekend. Who said city people don't have access to horses? You'd be surprised what a truly motivated individual could find when they have the horsey gene.

6   Human beings use voice a lot more than animals. Animals use body language about as much as we use language to communicate. Here is one exercise that uses simple body language which can help with a yappy dog who thinks he's the alpha. It exhibits how much more important body language and eye contact are with dogs. If you ever find your dog barks just too much, try to understand that he's trying to tell you something. Imagine him thinking the same thing about you (she just barks too much!). Maybe your dog is barking because someone's at the door. Maybe he's begging for his dinner or a snack. Maybe he's warning you about a snake in the yard. After ruling out the obvious, you might find that your dog is trying to usurp your power or usurp your alpha. There's always one alpha in every pack of animals. Without the secure sense of having another alpha animal taking charge, a dog may feel the need to step into the role of alpha and have to take charge. This is where you come in. If your dog doesn't trust you or respect you enough to be his leader, he'll always be trying to take charge. You need to recognize this. For the yappy dog who can't seem to stop barking, you need to enforce, and reinforce that you are the alpha, not him. Imagine this scenario. Your dog is in a playful mood, but you must attend to a chore. Your dog starts barking as if to say "No, give ME your attention." Study the look in his face. He's repeatedly saying "I am the alpha

over you." It's time to reverse that role for good. Stand straight up and look squarely at him with both hands on your hips. Don't move. Don't say a word, not a word. Just look at him with a very intent gaze, not an angry one, just stare at him. Try not to blink. You are sending him the body language sign, in no uncertain terms, that you will not put up with his behavior. He should get the message that his barking is inappropriate, but his reaction will come depending on how long you've had him as a pet and how long he has been used to his habit of barking. It could be immediate if he's sensitive, to a few minutes, but it will come: The look in his face will turn from "Hey, you, can't you hear that I'm trying to tell you something??" to "Hello there, anybody home" to "Sorry about that, I must have lost my mind for a moment." And he should stop barking and walk away. That is your goal. Several things can happen, though. He might actually start barking louder and with more assertiveness. He might actually jump up on you or against you. If he does that, he has over-stepped his limit and you must nip that behavior in the bud. Once again, say nothing, but step forward towards him. That in itself is an act of alpha aggression, as he has tried with you, but you must curtail his need to be the alpha. If he jumps up on you again, step towards him again. This is how another alpha animal would react, so that is how you must react. Use the opportunity of his assertiveness to turn the tables and re-assert your alpha.

7   A dog often looks at you when you work around his head. You might notice that the look in his face changes, especially if he doesn't know what's about to be done. His eyes might open wide, he might have a furrow in his brow, etc. If that happens, you will help him to relax if you squint. Yes, squint. Look at him with soft eyes and slowly close your eyes lightly and then open them. Then close one eye slowly, open, and close the other, then open. You are telling your dog through body language that you are relaxed and there's nothing to worry about. If you have previously established your alpha, then he will see that you are relaxed in this possible threat of new grooming. As you are the alpha and can be relaxed, he trusts you and so he will automatically relax as well. I've used this technique with all of my young puppies in their first grooming while they are lying on their backs in my lap. They often look up to me as they've never been groomed before, seemingly uncertain of this grooming thing. As they see me slowly close my eyes as if I'm going to sleep and relax my shoulders down, maybe dropping my head down a little, I can easily feel their anxious little bodies soften in my lap. Their eyes also start to droop and some actually fall asleep.

8   One practice I've seen repeatedly by horseback riders is The Smack. It has always bothered me that some riders praise their horse for doing a good job by smacking the side of their neck very hard and repeatedly, usually after departing from an obstacle successfully jumped. Really? What horse enjoys being really slapped hard on its neck? That must really sting. Obviously the rider is not considering his horse's feelings. I believe any horse would better appreciate a good, deep scratching on their mane, the top of the neck just in front of their shoulder. It's the natural, secret itchy spot all horses love. You often see horses grooming each other in a pasture, neck to neck, one scratching the other right there as it's getting scratched on the neck to the obvious delight of both. The next time you get to know a horse on your own, try scratching into that part of their neck. Watch the horse's facial expression change. My horses often curl their necks to the side while lifting their heads and extending out their top lip as if to say, "Ah, yes, that's it, ooh, a little to the side. Thank you!"

9   Routinely, dogs are trained on the leash as they remain on the left side of their trainer. For the purposes of this book, since you will be training your dog like a horse, you will learn how to keep him at your right side. Keep in mind that horses are mostly led around or mounted from the horse's left side. It's called the near side of

a horse, and the far side is their right side. Also, some people lead horses as they stand right next to the horse's head. However, this is not the safest place as you can't read the body language of your horse's ears or his intentions. More safe is the position just to the left side of a horse's shoulder, but with a foot or two away from the horse, out of your personal space. That way you could assess a horse's response before he responds.

10 If you only work on one side of an animal, they get used to it and could become one-sided, and stiff on the other side. Horses in particular must be trained on both sides as that's just how their brain works. Don't assume that just because you can touch him everywhere on his left side that he will be used to the same spots you touch on his right side. Thoroughbred racehorses are notorious for being easier to be handled and ridden on the left side and while making left-hand turns. It's because that's how they were mostly handled in their training. Some horses have to be specially retrained on their right side to relearn what they already know on their left. Working on both sides of an animal will also help you to become more versatile, and not so one-sided yourself. Many horseback riders are stronger on one side, which can actually cause a horse to move unbalanced.

11 I've seen some horseback riders ask a horse to move forward by kicking them in the ribs which means go, but at the same time pulling back on the horses' reins, which means stop to the horse. The poor horse is confused – "Should I walk or should I stay still?" With some horses, this can also become dangerous as some riders try to bully their horses, strongly kicking while strongly pulling back. The only option left for the horse is to move straight upwards, or rear. If a horse reared in that situation, it's only exactly what the rider was asking for. If the rider kicks the horse, the rider is telling the horse to move forward, but jerking back hard on the reins means move that energy backward. Naturally, there's nowhere for both forward and backward energy to go but up, so a horse explodes upwards in a rear, standing on his legs. Unfortunately, a rider may not see this coming. If the rider made his commands more clear, the horse would have moved forward just by being nudged a little with the rider's legs, and a horse will stop if the reins are gently pulled back. Keep your commands clear.

12 Of interest is how horses physically show that they think. I call it watching the dashboard gauges: Watching their ears. Their ears could indicate how they are feeling or where they are looking, even what they are about to do. If you ever get to see a horse move, check out

which direction his ears move. Are they pointed straight out front? This could mean they are intently focused right in front of them and are alert. If one ear is pointed forward and one ear to the side, the side-pointed ear means their focus just shifted to that side. If both ears are floppy and lazy looking, a horse is very relaxed, maybe apathetic or very tired. If their ears are "pinned" straight back, you can be pretty sure they're angry about something or are trying to warn either another horse or you to get out of their way.

13 I remember as a child having what I considered a really great lesson in jumping in an arena. The horse assigned to me was a very good jumper and really liked that job, but didn't like trail riding so much. We had just finished quite a long and somewhat tiring round of jumping in the arena. We usually cooled down our horses with a trail ride. My horse wasn't keen on going out on the trail that day. He just wanted to go back to the barn, but did what I asked him anyway. As we rode out onto the trail, I took off my hardhat as it was a hot summer day. My horse kind of dragged his feet, and as he did, he tripped onto the hard dirt pavement. It happened in a split second, which made me fly off and land on my face. It knocked me out and I still have a scar on my shoulder to this day. It was actually dangerous for me to not be alerted

to the boredom in my horse, and further it was downright stupid for me to take off my hardhat while still riding the horse. Never compromise safety.

14 This company actually makes custom tack for small animals. braymere@comcast.net

15 There is very good reason to post on the "correct diagonal." The horse's outside, front leg does a bit more work than the inside, front leg. If you post correctly, you will be up and out of your saddle as that outside, front leg does its thing, that is travel and be placed properly, allowing the horse to be balanced and yet traveling with an unrestricted shoulder over the ground. If you are up and out of the saddle, you are allowing your horse to move at its best with that harder-working outside leg.

16 I remember distinctly when I arrived at that moment. I had asked Bambi to jump over one of the long sheet metal ducts I borrowed from my father's shop. It was 2 feet tall with a span of 2 feet. Keeping in mind that little Bambi weighed only 10 pounds, and at 12 inches tall, this would have been the equivalent of jumping a horse over a 10-foot jump. So far, the world record for the highest a horse has ever jumped is 8 feet 1-1/4 inches. Obviously, I was asking too much of Bambi, and he refused the jump. Had he jumped

it, he could have hurt himself. I assumed that he was fit enough to take the jump since I had been regularly working with him for months, but he just knew better. I agreed to stop at less than that height with him.

17 Whenever leading a horse through a gate, you should go through the gate first, leading your horse behind you. Never push a horse through a gate first as he could rip the lead rope out of your hand, or push you into the narrow side of the door, etc. Also in turning a horse out into a pasture, you should open the gate, go through the pasture gate yourself first while leading your horse behind you, turn your horse back around, facing you and the gate, close the gate, and then remove the horse's halter/lead rope. Never smack a horse on the behind or scare him to run out to the pasture as he will develop the bad habit of turning in a microsecond while you are still attached to that rope and bolt off into the pasture, taking you with him. Some other spoiled horses can turn around very quickly and accurately kick out at you in their zeal to get out in the pasture. Insist on good manners with your horse in going through any gate.